**Political Development and
Bureaucracy in Libya**

Political Development and Bureaucracy in Libya

Omar I. El Fathaly
Arab Development Institute

Monte Palmer
Florida State University

Richard Chackerian
Florida State University

Lexington Books
D.C. Heath and Company
Lexington, Massachusetts
Toronto

Library of Congress Cataloging in Publication Data

el Fathaly, Omar.
    Political development and bureaucracy in Libya.

    Includes index.
    1. Libya—Politics and government. I. Palmer, Monte, joint author.
II. Chackerian, Richard, joint author. III. Title.
JQ3595.A1F37   309.1'61'204   77-712
ISBN 0-669-01426-5

Copyright © 1977 by D. C. Heath and Company

All rights reserved. No part of this publication may be reproduced or transmitted in any form or by any means, electronic or mechanical, including photocopy, recording, or any information storage or retrieval system, without permission in writing from the publisher.

Published simultaneously in Canada

Printed in the United States of America

International Standard Book Number: 0-669-01426-5

Library of Congress Catalog Card Number: 77-712

Contents

	List of Tables	vii
	Acknowledgments	ix
Chapter 1	Introduction	1
Part I		7
Chapter 2	Libya: The Social, Economic, and Historical Milieus *Omar I. El Fathaly*	9
	Social Environment	9
	Economic Environment	15
	Political Environment	21
	Summary	27
Chapter 3	The Impact of Sociopolitical Change on Economic Development in Libya *Omar I. El Fathaly* and *Fathi S. Abusedra*	33
	Socioeconomic History	33
	Conclusion	42
Part II		45
Chapter 4	Political Development among Rural Libyans *Omar I. El Fathaly* and *Monte Palmer*	47
	Methodology	48
	Some Theoretical Comparisons of Traditional and Modern Societies	48
	Rural Libya as a Traditional Society	51
	Political Development among Rural Libyans	58
	A Comparison of the Political Attitudes of Rural and Less Rural Populations	69
Chapter 5	Opposition to Social Change among Traditional Libyan Elites *Omar I. El Fathaly* and *Monte Palmer*	75
	Methodology	77
	Traditional Elites in Libya: A Profile	78
	The Legitmacy of Traditional Elites: The View from Below	79

	Tradition and Change among Local Elites	83
	Summary and Conclusions	87
Chapter 6	**Leadership, Institutionalization, and Mass Participation in Libya** *Omar I. El Fathaly* and *Richard Chackerian*	91
	Research Procedures	92
	Modernizing Leaders, Institutions, and the Public	92
	Popular Committee Leadership, Institutions, and the Public	96
	The People's Congress, Workers' Unions, ASU Leadership, and the Public	99
	Conclusion	101
Part III		103
Chapter 7	**From Bureaucratic to Open Systems: Models of Development Administration** *Richard Chackerian*	105
	The Struggle to Preserve Bureaucracy as a Model of Development Administration	105
	The Open-Systems Perspective: The Centrality of Exchange and Equifinality	109
	Environments of Open Systems: Certainty and Stability	110
	Changing Objectives and Changing Administrative Strategies: An Open-Systems Perspective	111
Appendix A	**Declaration of the Establishment of the People's Authority**	117
	Index	119
	About the Authors	123

List of Tables

2-1	Number of Students Enrolled in All School Levels in Libya between 1958-1959 and 1973-1974	14
2-2	Libyan Total Revenue and the Contribution of Oil Revenue to Total Revenue	17
3-1	Oil Production and the Contribution of Oil Revenue to Total Revenue	35
3-2	Ordinary and Development Budgets from 1963-1964 to 1976-1977	36
3-3	Allocations among Sectors in the 1973-1975 Plan	37
3-4	Five-Year Development Plan Allocations by Sector	38
4-1	Religiosity among Rural Libyans	52
4-2	Particularism among Rural Libyans	54
4-3	Atomistic Attitudes among Rural Libyans	55
4-4	Fatalism among Rural Libyans	55
4-5	Interpersonal Distrust among Rural Libyans	56
4-6	Tribalism among Rural Libyans	57
4-7	Leadership Preference among Rural Libyans	59
4-8	Evaluations of Mayors by Rural Libyans	61
4-9	Evaluations of Local and Provincial Administrations by Rural Libyans	62
4-10	Levels of Support for Government Reform and Welfare Measures	64
4-11	Rural Participation in Government Modernization Programs	67
4-12	Political Participation among Rural Libyans	68
4-13	Information Exposure and Support for Political Modernization	71
5-1	Preferred Attributes of Traditional Rural Elites	80
5-2	Education and Declining Support for Traditional Elites	82
5-3	Change Predispositions among Rural Libyan Elites	84

5-4	Contrasting Perceptions of Community Needs	85
5-5	Receptivity of Traditional Rural Elites to the Value of Economic and Social Development	86
5-6	Attitudes of Traditional Rural Elites toward Modernizing Administrators	87
6-1	Modernizing Leaders' Exposure to Media	94
6-2	Public Perception of Mayors' Attitudes toward Community Participation	95
6-3	Educational Levels of Traditional Leaders, Public, Popular Committee Members, and the Modernizing Leaders	98
6-4	Evaluations of the Modernizers by Popular Committee Members	99

Acknowledgments

The authors wish to thank the innumerable individuals in Libya and the United States who contributed to the success of the research described herein. We wish to express our special appreciation to Mr. Shahati, Secretary of Foreign Relations of The Peoples General Congress and to The Arab Development Institute for their support of the project. Errors of all variety are the sole responsibility of the authors. We share equally in them.

**We wish to dedicate this book to
Ibrahim El Fathaly**

1 Introduction

Independent Libya came into existence on December 24, 1951, following several centuries of Ottoman control, three decades of Italian occupation, and almost a decade of British and French administration. The Libyan Arab Republic, known as the Kingdom of Libya until the Socialist revolution of 1969, consists of three separate states: Tripolitania (Tripoli), Cyrenaica (Benghazi), and Fezzan, with a combined area of about 680,000 square miles. As such Libya is the fourth largest state in Africa, yet possesses a total population of just over two and one-half million people.

Libya's brief history as an independent state reads much like a tale from Arabian Nights. Born a poor orphan in the wake of World War II, Libya was described by Benjamin Higgins as the

> prototype of poor country . . . the bulk of the people lived on a subsistence level . . . no sources of power and no mineral resources, where agricultural expansion is severly limited by climate conditions, where capital formation is zero or less, where there is no skilled labor supply and no indigenous entrepreneurship. . . . Libya is at the bottom of the range in income and resources.[1]

Following the discovery of massive oil resources in the late 1950s, Libya was dramatically transformed by its petroleum wealth into one of the richest nations on earth. Per-capita income in 1977, for example, is estimated to be more than $5,178.

Wealth in itself, however, does not produce economic or political modernization. As the early history of Libya's oil boom well illustrates, excessive and unguided wealth tends to generate corruption, political conflict, waste, massive urban migration, dependency on the government, and the decay of the agrarian sector.

Indeed, Mohammed Heikal, the former editor of *Al Ahram*, may have had Libya in mind when he suggested that certain Arab oil states "had moved from nomads on to corruption without passing through civilization."

Analyses of Libya's economic structure recommend that her massive but finite oil revenues be utilized to dramatically broaden the base of the Libyan economy, with particular stress being placed upon the modernization of agriculture and the development of light industries congruent with her resources and market base.

In line with such recommendations, Libya's revolutionary leaders drastically reordered the economic priorities established by the monarchy, placing strong emphasis on the development of the agrarian sector, the development and diversification of industry, and the general lessening of the dependence of her economy on oil production. The current economic development plan, for example, projects, perhaps optimistically, that petroleum production will account for less than 50 percent of Libya's national income by 1980.

Similar transformations have been projected in the social arena. Recent laws provide for the mandatory education of children under the age of sixteen and compulsory adult education programs for individuals in selected occupations. Tribal status, once the basis of administrative districts, has been abolished. Health care, housing, and education are guaranteed to all Libyans.

However ambitious in scope, the success of the government's goals for the economic and social transformation of Libya depend, ultimately, upon its ability to develop politically. One clear dimension of political development in the Libyan context relates to the ability of Libya's revolutionary leaders to develop political institutions capable of initiating and executing incredibly complex social and economic modernization programs. Of particular importance in this regard is the ability of the leaders to develop a cadre of administrative personnel at the regional and local levels dedicated to the values of social and economic modernization and capable of penetrating Libya's predominantly rural and very traditional population. Unless regional and local officials share the modernization values of the revolutionary leadership, it is unlikely that they will pursue the modernization programs outlined by the central government with the dedication and enthusiasm that their successful implementation clearly demands. By the same token, unless the administrators charged with the implementation of Libya's social and economic development can penetrate and gain the confidence of her predominantly rural masses, their ability to sell the government's modernization programs to the population will be minimal and the modernization programs will likely fall victim to confusion and stagnation. If Libyans are to be mobilized in support of social and economic modernization and persuaded to give the modernization programs the opportunity to demonstrate their utility, it is essential that they possess at least minimal faith in their political institution.

A second dimension of political development involves the ability of Libya's revolutionary leaders to legitimize their modernizing institutions. The legitimization process involves at least four steps: (1) a reduction in mass support for the traditional tribal elites that provided the foundation of Libya's "ancient regime" and that are presumed to be hostile to modernization; (2) the emergence of an awareness and positive evaluation of the very substantial efforts made by the revolutionary leaders to improve the standard of living of all Libyans; (3) the development of a willingness on the part of Libya's predominantly rural population to trust and cooperate with modern oriented administrative personnel;

and (4) the willingness of the population to actively participate in the political system, to join its political organizations, and to get involved in its modernization programs.

Clearly, the more Libya's revolutionary leaders are able to develop an institutional framework capable of efficiently pursuing their goals of economic and social modernization and the greater the receptivity of Libya's predominantly rural populations to their newly created institutions, the more successful and rapid the process of economic development is likely to be.

The six studies that comprise this volume examine various facets of political development in revolutionary Libya. In particular, they examine the revolutionary government's pragmatic and often painful search for an institutional framework capable of facilitating the social, economic, and political transformation of Libya, the attitudes and values of the individuals who must administer the massive modernization programs, and the attitudes of the public toward their political institutions and administrators. Indeed, a majority of the studies are based upon the results of a broad sample survey designed to assess the political values of the Libyans as well as their attitudes toward political and economic reform. The same project also included a parallel survey of traditional tribal elites, local administrators, and members of Libya's recently instituted People's Committees. Specific descriptions of the methodologies employed in the survey will be outlined.

In terms of format, the contributions to this volume fall into three logical segments. Part I (consisting of Chapters 2 and 3) provides an extensive overview of Libyan society and describes their political and economic systems as they existed under the monarchy. Part I also briefly outlines the political and economic aspirations of the revolutionary government. Part II, consisting of Chapters 4, 5, and 6, utilizes the sample survey to evaluate Libya's progress in developing a political framework capable of executing the complex social and economic transformation envisioned by the revolutionary leaders. Chapter 4, for example, examines the extent to which Libya's predominantly rural population continues to support traditional tribal elites, recognizes government effort to improve their standard of well-being, is willing to trust and cooperate with local administrators, and has or has not become politically involved with the Libyan government. Chapter 3 also examines the extent to which Libya's better educated and more urban citizens are more supportive of political and economic modernization than their more traditional counterparts. Chapter 4, in turn, examines the political values of the traditional tribal elites that formed the backbone of the monarchy in an effort to ascertain the extent that traditional elites are, indeed, unalterably opposed to political and economic modernization or whether they might profitably be co-opted into the modernization process. This is an important question, for as the discussion in Chapter 4 indicates, support for the traditional tribal leaders remains strong among the rural segments of the population.

Building upon the discussion in Chapters 4 and 5, Chapter 6 outlines and evaluates the dramatic structural changes in the Libyan political system that have been initiated by the revolutionary regime in an effort to create efficient political institutions capable of leading the socialist modernization of Libya.

Finally, in Part III, Chapter 7, Professor Chackerian places the experience of Libya's institutional development in the context of the recent theoretical models of public administration.

A Methodological Note

The data for the six studies which comprise the volume have been drawn from a wide variety of sources. The background materials presented in Chapters 1 and 2, for example, utilize the few published works on Libya and materials developed by recent Ph.D. dissertations. The chapters also utilize a variety of government documents and rely heavily on the personal experience of Dr. El Fathaly. Material relating to the Popular Revolution and recent institutional changes in the structure of the political system are the result of research conducted by Dr. Omar I. El Fathaly during 1975 and 1976 while serving as Director of Political Research at the Arab Development Institute, a position he continues to hold.

The attitudinal data presented in Chapters 3, 4, and 5 are the result of a sample survey orally administered in the province of Zavia during the summer and fall of 1973. The details of the survey are presented at this point to save needless repetition in the papers that form the substantive chapters of the book.

The initial draft of the survey instrument was developed in the United States in English. Later it was translated to Arabic and pretested at the University of Libya-Benghazi. An interview team of forty-nine students from the University of Libya and the Zavia Teacher's Institute were given one week of training. After the training session, the interviewers were divided into teams based primarily on common tribal origins. It was felt that the refusal rate would be high if the interviewers were not native to the area in which the interviews were to take place. It was also necessary that each interviewer be given authorization by the ministry of interior. Letters of authorization from the ministry of interior were particularly important in gaining the cooperation of municipal officials.

The general survey contained four distinct subsamples: municipal and provincial officials ($n = 21$), popular committee members, ($n = 60$), tribal leaders, ($n = 14$), and general public, ($n = 576$). The sample of public officials included the mayors, deputy mayors, and the department heads of the seven municipalities of Zavia province. The popular committee sample included municipal level popular committee directors and deputy directors in Zavia province as well as a random sample of popular committee members.

INTRODUCTION

In selecting respondents for the approximately 600 public interviews, a quota was assigned to each of the seven municipalities in the province based upon their population. Within each municipality, respondents were selected by using a stratified random sample. Every municipality is divided into zones headed by a zone administrator. The head of the interview team contacted the mayor of the municipality to identify the zone administrator. The zone administrator provided information on the total number of people in the zone and the geographic locations within the zone of major social groups such as government employees, small businessmen, farmers and bedouins. The zone random sample was clustered within each of these major social groups because there is no documentation that would allow random identification of geographic areas within zones. The sampling strategy was to identify major social and geographic clusters (government employees at work, farmers on their farms, small businessmen in their shops, and bedouins in their geographic areas) and randomly select a quota from each cluster. The size of the sample from each of these clusters was based on the zone administrator's estimate of the relative size of the group in the zone.

One way to check the accuracy of a sample is to examine the extent to which its demographic characteristics correspond to known demographic characteristics of the population.

In this regard the public sample is drawn from the male population nineteen years and older. Females were excluded because they participate in the political process at very low rates (an estimated 3 percent turnout at the last provincial election) and when they do participate it usually follows the pattern of husbands or fathers. Males under nineteen were excluded because that is the legal age for electoral participation. The proportion of males nineteen and older in the sample corresponds quite closely to the proportion in municipalities of Zavia. The largest discrepancy is in Zahara (11 percent in the population and 16 percent in the sample). In the remaining six municipalities the difference is no greater than 3 percent. Zavia province, with 24 percent of the population male and nineteen years or older, closely corresponds to the 27 percent for the entire country.

To ascertain the reliability of the questionnaire, responses to three Likert-type items of similar content were examined for the percentage of response incongruence. Extreme response incongruence (shifts of more than one position) totaled less than 4 percent among the public respondents. Extensive shifting, however, did occur among adjacent positions, a fact in large measure explained by the slightly different emphasis of the items involved in the reliability correlations. Virtually no response incongruence occurred among the more specialized subsamples in reference to items of similar content. Content validity was the major validity control used in the study. The validity of the questionnaire was also ascertained by extensive pretesting in Libya and by the evaluation of the questionnaire by a panel of Libyan scholars and administrators. Ambivalent items were either deleted or revised.

Notes

1. Benjamin Higgins, *Economic Development: Problems, Principles and Policies* (revised edition; New York: W.W. Norton and Company, 1968), p. 26.

Part I

2

Libya: The Social, Economic, and Historical Milieus
Omar I. El Fathaly

It is difficult to discuss the political development of any society without first surveying the social, economic, cultural, and historical milieus in which the process of political development must occur. It is the objective of this chapter to provide reasonably detailed descriptions of those of Libya.

Social Environment

The basic units of Libyan society are the extended family, the clan, the tribe, and the village, with some modification of this arrangement in urban centers. Each plays a major role in the individual's and community's life and perception.

The typical Libyan family is an extended family consisting of father, mother, single and married sons, unmarried daughters, grandparents, grandchildren, uncles, aunts, and cousins. The father or oldest male is usually the top authority in the family. (Adult status is usually bestowed on fathers.) Sons carry on the name of the family and return to the father's house. Daughters keep their original family name but belong to their husband's family as long as they are married.

The individual in a traditional society like Libya's subordinates his personal interests to those of his family and considers himself to be a member of a group whose importance outweighs his own.[1] Since the individual is identified with his family, his good or bads deeds bring collective fame or shame to the family and to the tribe. It is the family unit that integrates virtually every aspect of the individual's life: social, economic, and political. It is the family "which socializes the individual into his culture and which bears primary responsibility for his adherence to social norms."[2]

Family membership is also a requirement, in most cases, for membership in larger units like clans and tribes. The family, as well as the clan and the tribe, functions as the educational, economic, and security providing organization for its members. The high degree of collectiveness and solidarity cannot be matched in any modern organization. In return, the individual has to obey, respect, and preserve the rules and traditions of those social units.

Related families constitute the clans and the tribe. Usually, leadership of the tribe belongs to the head or members of the most powerful family within the most powerful clan, although occasionally the formal leader (sheikh or chief) of the tribe may be a member of a less powerful family who is backed by prominent families.

The power, prestige, and influence enjoyed by families in the social structure are due to multiple sources: (1) birth, that is, descent from leaders or reputable families, even after the disappearance of the original leaders, (2) individual or collective wealth, (3) size of family, clan, or tribe, which bring security and support, (4) religiousness, courage, and generosity, of the individual or the related group, (5) political or administrative position, and (6) power and prestige associated with the professional stature of lawyers, doctors, judges, and others, whose professions require a high level of education.[3]

The idea of family influence has been utilized by the national leadership as a source of control and mobilization, and functions as a link between national authority and citizens. The so-called ayan (notables), wujaha (influentials), or abna-el-ayelate (the sons of predominant families), took the roles of leadership in Libyan society from the period of Ottoman control up to the 1969 revolution.

The Hierarchy of Traditional Authority

Decision making in a traditional society like Libya's is highly authoritative. Heads or chiefs of social units, in consultation with some of the elders in those units, make the decision. Kinship and unit solidarity provide the support of the rest of the unit members necessary to carry out those decisions. Failure to carry them out would threaten the solidarity and communal brotherhood, an eventuality which would challenge the very existence of the traditional individual.

The same roles of hierarchy, kinship, and collective solidarity are at play in the selection of leaders in traditional Libyan society. Within the immediate unit, the family, all authority and leadership belong to the father, grandfather, or eldest son. These authorities demand absolute loyalty from family members. To act contrary to familial leadership is to commit treason and is treated as such. The decisions of the leaders must be respected and carried out by all the members.

In the second unit, the clan, leadership is based on the prestige, reputation, and economic and social status of the family. A family that scores high on these ascriptive factors has greater power and influence, as well as a more favorable chance to assume the leadership of the clan. Selection of leadership in the third unit, the tribe, is subject to the same conditions, except that at this level the family that assumes the position of leadership builds reputation and power for the whole clan to which it belongs. Likewise, special status will rest on a tribe when one of its families assumes the leadership of the village, town, or region. Thus, collective identity of the family extends to the tribal level.

A family that has assumed a position of leadership on any level will find it hard to change its role or degrade its status. The inheritance of family status will continue from one generation to the next, preserving the reputation for a very long period of time. The fact that "several families controlled the country and determined the destiny of its people throughout the period of 1952 to 1969, then, was a logical result of the structure of Libyan society."[4]

Wherever there is competition for leadership or political position among tribes, the support for the candidates will split along tribal lines. The saying *weld kapeletna* ("the son of our tribe") will be the slogan of the supporters. *Weld bladna* ("the son or our village") will be the slogan when the range of competition is wider. *Weld ayla or bate* ("the son of family") implies more or less certain qualifications such as respectability, trustworthiness, righteousness, courage, religiousness, wealth, and belonging to a highly reputable family and tribe. Education, ability, and effectiveness are virtually invisible to the electorate.

Religion

Standing next in importance to the traditional units of family, clan, and tribes, religion is another variable that significantly affects the structure, values, and attitudes of Libyan society. It is a primary unit of loyalty and identity.

A religious title has its own connotation within the society. The *mufti* ("juris consult," or the top of the religious hierarchy) "held the highest honorary religious position in the country."[5] *Kodat* ("judges"), connected in the public mind with religion, enjoy exceptional privileges in the community. *Fakih* and *shaikh* ("religious teacher") were titles given to individuals exceptionally knowledgeable and wise in religious and general affairs. *Ulama* ("most knowledgeable," or "scientist") is a title given to the most erudite individuals, mainly in religious sciences and Islamic teachings.

The religious institutions and their leaders have played an important role in the social, educational, and political life of the country and its people. This role has a deep-rooted background, starting from the Ottoman occupation and continuing up to very recent days. The most notable and prolonged effects of religion have been on the leadership and institutions that regulate society. The judicial system, and many special and important political committees and advisory councils, for example, were dominated by notable religious leaders.

Throughout Libya's history and particularly under the monarchy, religion became a political symbol of crucial importance in controlling and mobilizing the masses. Religion, for example, was central to Arab League efforts to motivate the Libyan public to demand independence from the United Nations Commission. A *fatwa* ("declaration") was published, insisting that "voting for other than independence would be against religion."[6] As another example, the leaders of the National Congress party in making their bid for national leadership on the eve of Libyan independence in 1953 appealed to the masses, saying that their party was the true Islamic party. They stood for the unity of Islam and against federalism (the program of opposition), which was for the division of Islam and yielding to the infidels.[7]

There was inevitable association between family prominence and religious leadership. This fact served to intensify the concentration of religious leadership within small groups of families throughout the country. The strong role of religion in a traditional Islamic society like that of Libya has produced a society with special features. Conservative attitudes have been predominant in every respect. People's values and behavior have been a function of their religious background and attachment; hence, evaluation and acceptance of innovation and change has been subject to religious beliefs and notions. Libyans have looked to the Koran as a source of and guide for right action. The supreme laws have been the laws of God, which determine their relations with each other and with God.

Education

Throughout the Ottoman period, the only centers of learning were religious institutions, located in only a small number of cities in Libya. Education was available to only a few individuals whose families recognized the value of education, or whose family economic condition allowed the children to be spared from work. The quality of education available, and the length of time one could spend as a student, were limited. The student could be trained as a teacher of the Arabic language or religious science, or as a *kadisharia* ("judge of Islamic jurisprudence").

During the Italian occupation, religious education continued to be the major type available. More Koranic schools were opened through private efforts, but instability of the region and severe economic conditions prevented this already inadequate system of education from flourishing. Secular schools were also opened in a few urban centers during this time. The policy of the colonial administration was to restrict the number of Libyans educated beyond the primary stage, and all teaching was conducted in Italian.[8] The handful of Libyans who wanted to seek further education had to travel to Egypt, where they could continue mainly in Arabic literature and religious science, or to Italy and a few other regions for study in more secular fields of knowledge.

The British administration put more emphasis on secular education and established vocational schools separate from religious educational institutions.

The new schools, still inadequate, with meager resources and teaching staff, served only residents of urban centers.

In general, the society was untouched by education, and even years after independence, "more than 90 percent of the population were illiterate and only a handful of Libyans had been given an opportunity to study at a university or to qualify for a recognized profession."[9] During the first decade of independence, severe economic problems, regional conflict of interests, and poor management of the available resources severely handicapped the development of a sound education system. On the eve of independence, of a total enrollment of 32,741, only 537 students were attending secondary and technical schools. There were no girls enrolled in secondary schools, and there were no female primary school teachers. The number of secondary school teachers totaled 25, and only 14 Libyans held university degrees from European and Egyptian universities.[10] Finally, not until 1959 were the first university degrees awarded to a graduating class of 31 by the only Libyan university.[11]

The discovery of oil at the beginning of the 1960s brought a radical change in the Libyan economy and eliminated the economic obstacle to education. Since then, educational facilities have greatly expanded, schools have been built in rural and remote areas, more colleges have been established in the University of Libya, and more vocational schools and training centers have been instituted.

Education during the monarchical period experienced much more influence from religious elements than in any of the previous periods. The fact that King Idris owed his political power to his religious background and leadership was an important factor in his reactivation of existing religious institutions and the development of new ones. Even with relatively large expansion, the educational system did not meet the country's need for trained technical, managerial, and skilled personnel.[12] The religious influence under the monarchical regime prevented a real assessment of the country's educational needs.

The revolutionary regime continued the quantitative expansion of the educational system, and has added tremendous changes in the quality and level of education. This regime has been trying to relate the educational system to current and future needs of the region. The most important changes in that direction are the following: (1) stress on vocational and technical training to provide the country with the most needed skills in such fields as agriculture, industry, and business; (2) a new trend in higher learning (college and graduate) toward applied sciences with immediate usefulness to the Libyan economy (engineering, petroleum industry, agriculture, medicine, electronics, and others); (3) an increase in the compulsory education period from six to nine years of successful schooling, and changes in the requirements and teaching methods at this level; (4) an expansion of the number and geographical distribution of schools and other educational institutions, in order to bring the rural and bedouin population in contact with education; (5) a merging between secular and religious education, for example, the amalgamation of the Islamic University with the University of Benghazi; and (6) a tremendous increase in adult education under new systems and rules.

Despite the tenfold increase in the student population in the period 1951 to 1968, it was found that only about 54 percent of children between six and eleven years of age were enrolled in the primary grades (one through six) in 1968. Also, about 8 percent of youngsters between fifteen and nineteen years of age were attending secondary schools.[13] The enrollment figures over the last fifteen years show a revolutionary increase, at least in absolute numbers (see Table 1).

Funds spent on education during the same period have also increased phenomenally. Government spending on education increased from $51,000,000 in 1969-1970 to $204,000,000 in 1974. Schools increased in number from 1,265 in 1968-1969 to 2,214 in 1973-1974.[14] However, higher levels of education have not experienced the same rapid growth. The high percentage of dropouts after the first grades of primary school affected the enrollment in higher levels. For example, less than 11 percent of the total number of students enrolled in primary schools go to preparatory, 2.4 percent to secondary, 0.09 percent vocational, 1.1 percent teacher institutions, and 1.5 percent reached university. The percentage distribution by level of education indicates a handicap in the education system. Of the total enrollment, 85.8 percent enrolled in primary, 9.2 percent in preparatory, 2.1 percent in secondary, 0.7 percent in vocational, 0.9 percent in teacher institutions, and 1.3 percent in higher education.[15]

Table 2-1
Number of Students Enrolled in All School Levels in Libya between 1958-1959 and 1975-1976

Year	Primary	Preparatory	Secondary	Vocational	Teaching Institution	University
1958-1959	98,063	5,058	N.A.	718	1,676	342
1961-1962	131,098	11,216	2,284	1,155	2,162	942
1963-1964	154,592	14,286	2,214	1,190	2,407	1,280
1965-1966	192,293	18,720	4,326	933	3,330	1,891
1967-1968	248,731	26,414	5,995	909	5,254	2,522
1969-1970	310,846	36,316	8,304	1,457	4,725	3,633
1971-1972	405,435	43,346	9,426	3,202	5,984	6,291
1973-1974	484,986	73,928	13,417	3,411	15,605	9,590
1975-1976	554,015	N.A.	18,158	3,584	21,377	11,117

Source: Data from 1958-1959 through 1973-1974 taken from Ministry of Planning, L.A.R., *Historical Study on the Development of Education in Libya from the Otoman Period until Present* (Tripoli: Government Printing Office, 1974), pp. 29-59; 1975-1976 data from *Ministry of Education*, Report, p. 11.

The low enrollment in vocational and technical schools is a great obstacle in the development of the region, and immediate action to increase the proportion is vital. Mass education is usually thought to play a role in both economic modernization and the process of political change.[16] Any development strategy will be impractical without adequate levels of education to support the implementation of such strategies. Libyan society has always been faced with severe shortages of skilled and trained people in every field. The problem has continued despite the tremendous increase, mainly because new needs have been appearing as a result of radical changes in the economic and social structure of the region.

Urbanization

The Libyan population remains predominantly rural; the urban sector is still very small although growing rapidly. In 1954 the urban population represented 22 percent of the total, 27 percent in 1964, and an estimated 35 percent in 1972. According to population projections by private consultants, the urban population will increase by more than 52 percent between 1969 and 1979.[17]

The recent urbanization in Libya has consisted of rural immigration to the two main urban centers, Benghazi and Tripoli, whose annual population growths have been reported as 7.0 and 6.5 percent, respectively.[18] This immigration was due to the anticipation of higher wages and immediate cash, in some cases, and to the lack of the facilities of modern life (education, communication, health, and services) in the rural areas.

This one-way movement has led to deterioration of the already deficient agricultural sector and has aggravated the conditions of housing, transportation, and other services which were already behind in meeting the needs of the original city dwellers in both cities. New ideas were passed along to the immigrants less easily than expected because of shortcomings in services and communication systems.

In Libya, at least, modernizing the rural areas is more important in every aspect than immigration to urban centers. Recent efforts have been made to create favorable environments in the rural areas and reverse the immigration movement.

Economic Environment

A study of the Libyan economy could be divided into three periods: 1951-1960, 1960-1969, and 1969-1975.

$108,800 in 1968." The last figure was not enough to pay for Libya's import of food for one-third of a single day."[28]

The term *rentier* state has been applied to nations with economic situations similar to that of Libya. In this context, rentier state refers to states that receive revenue from their raw material production and exportation, where this process has very little to do with their domestic economic growth. Other production is very insignificant. H. Mahdavy, in applying the rentier state model to Iran[29] showed that the danger facing those states is that, while some of their natural resources are being fully developed by foreign concerns and considerable government expenditures, the mass of the population may remain in a backward condition and the most important factors for long-term growth may receive little or no attention at all.

This dangerous situation fits Libya precisely. The International Bank for Reconstruction and Development (IBRD) mission to Libya reported in 1960 that the discovery of oil did not provide an easy or a complete solution to the problems of economic development. The old problems have remained, and oil has provided only the financial means of solving them.[30] Robert Mabro applied the rentier state model to Libya and showed that Libya the looted state suddenly became Libya the wealthy rentier state, but the economy remained dependent and underdeveloped. Revenues accrued directly to the government, not through any production, but from oil taxes which come from outside the economy. Government expenditures and development programs became totally dependent upon oil revenues. Consumption patterns became geared to the use of imported commodities. There were no links between the proceeds of production, effort, and incentive. The rentier state can achieve dramatic rises in per capita income without going through the social and organizational changes usually associated with the processes of economic growth.[31]

The monarchy dealt with the abundant petro-money by allocating 70 percent of it for development, and accordingly, the first five-year plan was drawn in 1963 and concentrated on building the foundation of economic development by stressing infrastructural projects. The plan allocated $746,000,000, to be increased to a total of $1,234,000,000. In 1968, the plan was extended for the fiscal year 1968-1969 to permit adequate preparation of the second plan and, at the same time, to give the administration another year to complete the unfinished projects. The first plan and its extension demonstrated, among many other things, the shortsightedness and poor planning and management capabilities of the government agencies.

The priorities of the first plan were as follows: public works, transportation and communication, electrification, and others which absorbed about 43 percent of the total actual allocations. The priorities for the sectors of housing, agriculture, education, industry, and health were 11, 10, 9, 5, and 4 percent of the actual total, respectively.[32] The moneys allocated for industry did not even carry this sector to the take-off stage. In addition, the traditional small

The low enrollment in vocational and technical schools is a great obstacle in the development of the region, and immediate action to increase the proportion is vital. Mass education is usually thought to play a role in both economic modernization and the process of political change.[16] Any development strategy will be impractical without adequate levels of education to support the implementation of such strategies. Libyan society has always been faced with severe shortages of skilled and trained people in every field. The problem has continued despite the tremendous increase, mainly because new needs have been appearing as a result of radical changes in the economic and social structure of the region.

Urbanization

The Libyan population remains predominantly rural; the urban sector is still very small although growing rapidly. In 1954 the urban population represented 22 percent of the total, 27 percent in 1964, and an estimated 35 percent in 1972. According to population projections by private consultants, the urban population will increase by more than 52 percent between 1969 and 1979.[17]

The recent urbanization in Libya has consisted of rural immigration to the two main urban centers, Benghazi and Tripoli, whose annual population growths have been reported as 7.0 and 6.5 percent, respectively.[18] This immigration was due to the anticipation of higher wages and immediate cash, in some cases, and to the lack of the facilities of modern life (education, communication, health, and services) in the rural areas.

This one-way movement has led to deterioration of the already deficient agricultural sector and has aggravated the conditions of housing, transportation, and other services which were already behind in meeting the needs of the original city dwellers in both cities. New ideas were passed along to the immigrants less easily than expected because of shortcomings in services and communication systems.

In Libya, at least, modernizing the rural areas is more important in every aspect than immigration to urban centers. Recent efforts have been made to create favorable environments in the rural areas and reverse the immigration movement.

Economic Environment

A study of the Libyan economy could be divided into three periods: 1951-1960, 1960-1969, and 1969-1975.

The Period of the Artificial State (1951-1960)

At the time of independence Libya was one of the poorest nations in the world, with a per-capita income of less than $30 per year in 1951 and $100 per year in 1960. It was a prototype of a poor country "in the bottom of the range in income and resources," as Professor Higgins described it.[19] Over 70 percent of the labor force was engaged in agricultural and animal husbandry activities, which accounted for about 30 percent of the gross domestic product (GDP). Ironically, by the early 1970s agriculture accounted for only about 3 percent of the GDP and absorbed only about 30 percent of the labor force.[20] Of its vast area, only 5 percent was considered economically useful, and around 1 percent was regarded as susceptible to permanent cultivation. Because of the scarcity of ground water, the unreliability of rainfall, and the poor irrigation and production methods, the 1 percent was not economically utilized. The economic value of human resources, the known mineral resources, the available capital for development, and the climatic conditions were too poor to generate growth or provide any prospects for industrialization beyond certain traditional handicrafts.

These conditions gave little hope, if any, for Libyan economic and social development. To some experts, Libya was almost a hopeless case.[21] International donors participated in programs for technical and financial aid, and until the discovery of oil in 1959, Libya was greatly indebted for its economic and political viability to the United Nations and certain Western and Middle Eastern nations.[22]

The Period of Unmanageable Abundance (1960-1969)

The bleak picture of the first period changed rapidly and drastically with the oil discoveries in 1959. The outstanding characteristics of the Libyan economy within this period are the transformation of the country from stagnant to rapidly growing and control by the predominance of the oil sector. Within eight years of the first shipment, Libya became the world's fourth largest exporter of crude oil, a rate of growth unknown anywhere in the industry's history.[23]

Eventually, this dramatic change was reflected in the government budget and national economy. Surprisingly, within a few years, Libya moved from the status of a capital-deficit nation to a capital-surplus nation, from an aid recipient to an aid extender.[24]

The increase in oil revenue and its ratio to total revenue, accompanied by an unfortunate decrease in other sectors of the economy, especially agriculture, promoted over the first few years of this development the idea that oil is the key to the dynamic character of the Libyan economy and its vitality for the development of the region.[25] Table 2-2 dramatizes this condition. In addition,

$108,800 in 1968." The last figure was not enough to pay for Libya's import of food for one-third of a single day."[28]

The term *rentier* state has been applied to nations with economic situations similar to that of Libya. In this context, rentier state refers to states that receive revenue from their raw material production and exportation, where this process has very little to do with their domestic economic growth. Other production is very insignificant. H. Mahdavy, in applying the rentier state model to Iran[29] showed that the danger facing those states is that, while some of their natural resources are being fully developed by foreign concerns and considerable government expenditures, the mass of the population may remain in a backward condition and the most important factors for long-term growth may receive little or no attention at all.

This dangerous situation fits Libya precisely. The International Bank for Reconstruction and Development (IBRD) mission to Libya reported in 1960 that the discovery of oil did not provide an easy or a complete solution to the problems of economic development. The old problems have remained, and oil has provided only the financial means of solving them.[30] Robert Mabro applied the rentier state model to Libya and showed that Libya the looted state suddenly became Libya the wealthy rentier state, but the economy remained dependent and underdeveloped. Revenues accrued directly to the government, not through any production, but from oil taxes which come from outside the economy. Government expenditures and development programs became totally dependent upon oil revenues. Consumption patterns became geared to the use of imported commodities. There were no links between the proceeds of production, effort, and incentive. The rentier state can achieve dramatic rises in per capita income without going through the social and organizational changes usually associated with the processes of economic growth.[31]

The monarchy dealt with the abundant petro-money by allocating 70 percent of it for development, and accordingly, the first five-year plan was drawn in 1963 and concentrated on building the foundation of economic development by stressing infrastructural projects. The plan allocated $746,000,000, to be increased to a total of $1,234,000,000. In 1968, the plan was extended for the fiscal year 1968-1969 to permit adequate preparation of the second plan and, at the same time, to give the administration another year to complete the unfinished projects. The first plan and its extension demonstrated, among many other things, the shortsightedness and poor planning and management capabilities of the government agencies.

The priorities of the first plan were as follows: public works, transportation and communication, electrification, and others which absorbed about 43 percent of the total actual allocations. The priorities for the sectors of housing, agriculture, education, industry, and health were 11, 10, 9, 5, and 4 percent of the actual total, respectively.[32] The moneys allocated for industry did not even carry this sector to the take-off stage. In addition, the traditional small

Table 2-2
Libyan Total Revenue and the Contribution of Oil Revenue to Total Revenue

Year	Total Revenue (in million U.S. dollars)	Oil Revenue as Percentage of Total Revenue
1962	86.698	7.8
1963	121.050	20.0
1964	212.918	37.6
1965	289.027	63.6
1966	423.360	66.6
1967	1080.912	83.4
1968	838.320	76.5
1969	1205.904	77.4
1970	1491.840	82.0
1971	1853.177	84.9
1972	2840.076	88.4
1973	2459.772	85.3
1974	8619.240	95.3
1975	6999.290	95.1

Source: Volume 14 of *Annual Report: Bank of Libya*, Tripoli, 1970; Volume 17 of *Annual Report: Bank of Libya*, Tripoli, 1975; Volume 20 of *Annual Report: Bank of Libya*, Tripoli, 1975, pp. 114-116.

if the revenues generated from other activities connected with the oil industry are considered as part of the oil revenue, the contribution of oil to the total revenue is even greater.

Libya's society, administration, and economy were unprepared to utilize and absorb the new wealth. The effects of oil production on the economy were described by Dr. Ali Attiga, then Libya's Minister of Planning and Development.[26] He has shown that the rapid wave of one-way migration from rural areas to urban centers increased tremendously during this latter period. The result was crowded urban centers and deserted farmland in many parts of the country. As a result of increased urban population and increased per capita income, there was a sudden increase in the demand for food and agricultural products. This situation, given a healthy economy, could have been a strong stimulus to agricultural production. However, the low state of technological development in agriculture and the increasing cost of labor have resulted in reliance on agricultural imports, which increased over threefold during the sixties.[27]

"Libyan agriculture", explained Dr. Attiga, "was left to stagnate in its low level of development, and the consumer turned to the world markets for the purchase of his daily food. . . . At the beginning of oil exploration the total value of imported food and food produce was about $1,700,000. By 1969 it was $95,000,000." At the same time, agricultural exports had declined from a value of $4,180,000 in 1956 to "$2,040,000 in 1961, and to only about

industries and crafts began losing their consumer appreciation. In short, despite the tremendous increase in government revenues, and the exaggerated rate of growth of national income in this period (25 percent per year), and the enormous rate of increase in per capita income, which was "several times as high as the targets set in the more ambitious development programs of other countries."[33] the same fundamental problems of 1952 were still present.

Libya, according to Higgins, had become a prototype once again: no longer one of a poor country, it had become one of unbalanced growth. R. Mabro argued that there were essentially two ways in which Libya could use her oil to overcome the awesome disadvantages she had carried through history. One was to get more out of her oil by maintaining reasonable rates of oil extraction to prolong the life of oil resources in order to buy more time for development; the other was to concentrate on developing Libya's human capital as the sole key to real development. The monarchy failed on both counts.[34]

The Period of Abundance and Rushed Growth (1967-1975)

The First of September Revolution (1969) ended an era of international laissez-faire. At the same time, there were changes in the priorities of the development strategy. The goal of the new regime, from its very beginning, has been to change the situation of the rentier state from full dependence on oil to balanced growth among all sectors. The regime has particularly emphasized the creation of sound agricultural and industrial sectors at any cost.

In its transitional period, the attention of the new government has been focused on agriculture and agrarian reforms, which took around one-sixth of the budget. Industry had the second largest allocation. Communication, housing, utilities, and education followed in importance, respectively. The main accomplishment under the new regime has been the creation of government-owned and sponsored agricultural and industrial projects run by specialized government agencies. Another accomplishment has been the government partnership with the oil industry and other important activities. Nationalization, or "Libyanization" of certain industries or interests has begun in order to gain firmer control and supervision.[35] As can be plainly seen, the role of government has been tremendously increased.

The government implemented its first three-year development plan in 1973. Differences in priorities between the new and old regimes, determined by comparing sector allocations in the 1963-1968 plan with those in the 1973-1975 plan, indicated that the latter has placed more stress on agriculture, industry, and introduction of new sectors (petroleum and other minerals), as well as more money for electrification, housing, and public services.

The new regime increased petroleum prices, which provided abundant funds for every sector, particularly agriculture and industry. For agriculture the amount of money budgeted from 1971-1972 was five times as much as there had been in 1966, and the amount for industry was seven times as much. The increases of the 1973-1975 plans over the 1963-1968 plan, in agriculture and industry, are 8.5 percent and 15.5 percent, respectively.[36]

The target of the new plan was to achieve a maximum growth rate in real GDP, accompanied by a greater diversification in the structure of the economy. Positive action was taken to balance the national economy through the sincere efforts to build new productive sectors and lessen the dependence on oil. The nonoil sectors were expected to grow by 57.5 percent over the three-year span, while over the same period the oil sector will be allowed to grow by only 15.8 percent. Reasonable rates of crude oil extraction were maintained in order to prolong the life of the oil resources by applying conservation measures. Libya, the country within the Organization of Petroleum Exporting Countries (OPEC) most concerned with conservation measures, lessened its production by almost 21 percent, thereby giving itself more time for development and utilization of its oil resources. The new leadership has recognized that oil resources are depletable, and that alternative sources of revenues must be developed quickly if the country is to survive an expected "oil-less" future.

The new regime concentrated its efforts on redirecting and controlling the national economy. The Libyan government nationalized the country's banking, insurance, and petroleum marketing companies; there was expansion of participation in and control of industry and commerce by Libyans and Libyan-owned firms. In December 1971, the government nationalized the production and exporting facilities of the British Petroleum Company, and in the spring of 1972, it nationalized the pharmaceutical trade.[37]

By mid-1972, the government's role in the economy was overwhelming. Mineral and water rights were vested in the state. The basic infrastructural facilities — highways, communications, ports, airlines, electric power companies, major fishing facilities, postal services, agricultural farms, major industries, hospitals, and some trading companies — were directly or indirectly owned and operated by the government.[38]

The last two years (1974-1975) have witnessed great government expansion in agricultural activities and land reform. Hundred of thousands of acres were developed and made ready for production with all needed facilities. The Ministry of Agriculture and the Ministry of Agricultural Development, in addition to specialized independent agencies, were handling what is known as the "Agricultural Revolution," utilizing the best of international scientific know-how and technology.

When the new regime took over, Libya had virtually no industry. The few manufacturing enterprises in existence were mainly controlled by foreign investors. By April 1970, the government issued a decree which outlined its industrial policy. Large- and medium-scale industry, especially in the fields of oil, gas, agricultural processing, and construction materials, were to be reserved to the public sector. Industrial corporations run by the state were in charge of the public sector projects. Under the 1973-1975 plan, eighteen new factories have been under construction.[39] Textile factories were almost ready to produce by early 1975. There were three cement factories in production at this time, and two others were on the way. A steel industries complex was scheduled to start production by late 1975. Petrochemical and oil refining industries have begun production, and so have many other industries. M. J. Azoz, now the Minister of Industry, has concluded that the year 1975 is the year for industry in Libya. He forecast that the next five-year plan (1976-1980) will further hasten the pace of this industrial revolution.[40]

This boom has also brought to Libya the dilemmas of development and growth. Most of these problems are related to the shortage of labor, especially skilled labor; the inability of Libyan entrepreneurs to handle the development projects, the limited capacity of the local market to absorb future production, the public dependence and lack of participation in government, and a development process which was so rushed that neither time nor strength were sufficient to prepare or project properly. The pressure on the government to pursue development policies was tremendous. In the words of Major A. Jalloud, then minister in charge of production, "It was natural for any military group to produce economic and social plans for a radical change: so as to convince the people and the workers at large that it was not a movement aiming only at a seizure of power. This was the way army leaders could prove that they had led not a military coup d'etat but a revolution."[41] Even with some waste and misallocation, Libya's comfort is that we would be better off with those programs in a future with less oil than without them.

Political Environment

The Making of a State

Libya became an independent state under the auspices of the United Nations on December 24, 1951. Libya was divided into three states or provinces, Cyrenaica (Benghazi), in the east, Tripolitania (Tripoli) in the west, and Fezzan in the south. When the Italian occupation was replaced by the British Military Administration, the British authority promoted the ideas of independent Cyrenaica under "Emir" Idris, who had been proclaimed as Emir of Cyrenaica in 1921. No decision was made concerning Tripolitania or Fezzan. In the House of Commons' debates, Anthony Eden, then Secretary of State for Foreign Affairs, acknowledged that "His Majesty's Government is determined that at the end of the war [World War II] the Senussi [the king's family, tribe, followers] of *Cyrenaica* will in no circumstances again fall under Italian domination."[42] By the end of the war Idris and the notable leaders of Cyrenaica were more determined to seek independence under the leadership of Idris, and to be assisted and guided by Britain.

On behalf of Cyrenaica, Omar Mansur al-Kikhya, the most notable Cyrenaican leader after Idris, addressed a letter to Sir Edward Grigg, the British Minister of State in Cairo, asking the British to recognize Idris as the Emir of Cyrenaica, to recognize Cyrenaica as an independent country, and to assist Cyrenaica militarily, economically, and administratively. In return, Britain was to be given the right to station forces on Cyrenaican territory, and Cyrenaica was to be an ally of Britain.[43] On the same day, Idris endorsed al-Kikhya's proposals in a letter to Sir Grigg assuring that the proposals conformed "with our desires and the desires of our Cyrenaican nation."[44]

Tripolitanian leaders, with only meager cooperation of Fezzanan leaders, were trying to join Idris and his followers in a united front to make demands from the British. Tripolitania recognized the leadership of Idris but objected to the idea of an independent Cyrenaica, proposing instead the unity of the whole country. Al-Kikhya rejected Tripolitania's proposals and requested special treatment and status for Cyrenaica which the other part considered an "extravagant demand" and entirely unacceptable.[45]

With the signing of the Italian Peace Treaty in 1947 by the Big Four powers (United Kingdom, United States, USSR, and France), the fate of Libya and the other Italian colonies was left in the hands of the big powers, and finally the Libyan question was consigned to the United Nations. The Italians renewed hopes for their claim of sovereignty over Libya. Great Britain, ignoring its pledges of independence to the Libyans, as it did in the rest of the Middle East, joined Italy in the Bevin-Sforza Plan, named for Ernest Bevin and Count Carolo Sforza, the British and Italian foreign ministers. The plan suggested giving the United Nations trusteeship over Tripolitania, Cyrenaica, and Fezzan with Italy, Britain, and France, respectively, serving as trustees.[46]

The Libyan public and leadership responded violently with general strikes and demonstrations protesting the trusteeship plan. The rejection, which was both surprising and overwhelming, induced the support of Arab and Asian delegations to block the implementation of such a plan. The proposal was one vote short of the needed two-thirds majority. The role of the Haitian delegate, Emile Saint-Lot, who later became an honorary citizen of Libya, was crucial in the plan's defeat. Sforza, co-author of the plan, reacted by saying that "the sacrifices made by Italy in regard to her former African territories have failed to satisfy a majority composed mostly of delegations representing colored and small nations."[47]

The alternative plan of immediate independence was adopted by the General Assembly, and the process of making a new state began under the guidance and supervision of the United Nations. The Libyan leaders, although they recognized the leadership of Idris, still differed on the shape and position of their future state. One group, who preferred the unitary government with more ties and cooperation with the Arabs and less with the West, was organized by the National Congress Party under the leadership of Bashir al-Sa'dawi. A second group, led by Idris and the Independence party, sought a federal form of government as well as close relationships and allies in the West, especially with the United Kingdom and the United States. The outcome of a suspicious election favored the second group. The federal form of government was claimed by the eldest political leaders to provide a working scheme of integration between three separate and different states and peoples. From the nationalistic point of view, it was denounced as a preservation of influence and prestige of traditional leaders over the state. The latter were the king's most loyal supporters, and he took pains to appoint or promote them to key positions of federal and provincial leadership.[48]

The King and the Royal Diwan

Mohammed Idris El Senussi, the first king of the new kingdom of Libya, was born on March 12, 1890, in the remote oasis of Jaghbub, to an extremely religious family. His grandfather had founded the Senussi order which preached a return to the Islamic rituals and teachings as embodied in the Koran. Idris was educated in Islamic law and theology in the secluded Koranic School of Jaghbub.

Idris became a leader within the hierarchy of the Senussi order and family, and he enjoyed high prestige and power among tribal and religious elements, especially within the eastern part of the country. His political leadership derived from his role as a religious leader. Also, his exile in Egypt surrounded him with other leaders and notables who had fled the country during Italian occupation and who trusted and respected him for his family ties, religious background, and personality.

After the making of the state, the constitution granted the king broad powers: "the executive power shall be exercised by the king within the limits of the constitution" (Art. 42), and "legislative power shall be exercised by the king in conjunction with Parliament" (Art. 41). He opened and closed parliamentary sessions and could convene extraordinary sessions, and "when Parliament is not in session ... the king may issue decrees ... which shall have the force of law ..." (Arts. 62, 64). He created and conferred titles, namely the prime minister diplomatic representatives and senior officials, and could remove them from office at any time (Arts. 71-74). He appointed the members of the Senate (Art. 94). He was the supreme commander of all the armed forces and had the power to declare war, conclude peace, and enter into treaties which he ratified after the approval of Parliament (Arts. 65-69). The king, as "supreme head of the state," was "inviolable" and "exempt from all responsibilities" (Arts. 58-59).[49]

Idris devoted most of his energy to religious and tribal matters, and regretted the need to spend so much time on affairs of state.[50] Neither willing to delegate authority nor trust others to run the state, he impeded even the most able people of his administration in executing the duties of their posts. The king was confused and reluctant in his political stands, and he rarely expressed support for any specific programs or took a clear-cut position on public issues.[51]

While King Idris expressed devotion to the whole nation and publicly eschewed any thoughts of his own regional and personal interests, he privately confessed different feelings to the American ambassador to Libya. "I had many teas, as well as luncheons with King Idris during the two and a half years I resided in his realm," wrote Mr. Villard. "The unfailing subject of interest to him was the past, present and future of Cyrenaica. Uppermost in his mind was the rebuilding of Benghazi."[52]

While the country was suffering from poverty and lack of funds, the king's government kept moving between two capitols, and later three, mainly to keep the balance of regional influence and interests. The king spent funds generously on matters related to religion or promoting his family's history and image: the Islamic University (University of Mohammed Iben Ali El Sannussi) in Beida and Jaghbub, the building of the new (third) capital Beida, where part of his family resided or were buried. Beida has been described by one writer as "the Brasilia of Libya, built from nothing to nothing."[53]

The king's interest in his family history went further than expected. Egyptian President Nasser, speaking anecdotally of King Idris after news of the Libyan coup reached Egypt, recalled an occasion when Egypt was in urgent need of money to buy arms. Nasser said, "I sent Hassan S. El-Kholi to see the king, and he promised to give us L.D. 20 million straight away on only one condition — that we should return to him a subha (rosary) which had been given by one of his ancestors to al-Azhar mosque and which he thought was still hanging there. I told El-Kholi to go to al-Azhar and collect the subha and take it to the king (which he did)."[54]

The king always emphasized the Libyan-Arab brotherhood and solidarity, but unless he was under tremendous pressure, he never exceeded this lip service. He blocked Libyan membership in the Arab League until 1953, and he always fell short of showing any positive support to the Arabs in the Middle East, even when it was to his advantage to do so. Instead, the king consistently pursued strong relationships with the West. His agreements with the United Kingdom and United States did not serve his ends, but served to a great extent to inflate the gap between king and government on the one hand, and between king and opposing public on the other.

The Royal Diwan, headed by loyal but unable traditional leaders, acted always as a filter to whatever information relating to the people reached the king, and these leaders could advise him according to their own interests and mentality. The Royal Diwan gained tremendous power in running state affairs and contributed greatly to the instability of the political system. The Royal Diwan controlled many things that the king did not care to run or never heard about. Its leadership was a clear representation of power for tribal, familial, and religious elements in Libyan politics.

Cabinet

The federal system and the palace policies led to a real crisis in government. Clashes of authority broke out between federal and provincial politicians a few months after independence. A quarrel within the royal family, lack of coordination among the four governments in the region, and deeply conflicting regional interests contributed to internal disunity and the political instability of the country. The first government was brought down and Muntasir, the first prime minister, was forced to resign before the end of 1953 even though the king did not accept his resignation until February 1954.[55] The new cabinet, under the premiership of M. al-Sakisli, fell within two months as a result of conflict over the authority, jurisdiction, and legal boundaries of each government's bodies.[56]

The third cabinet, with M. Bin Halim as premier, survived for thirty-seven months, with a total of five cabinet reshuffles. Bin Halim faced tremendous regional conflicts and power struggles between his office and the Royal Diwan. Successor Abdu-al-Majid Kubar's cabinet was brought down in 1960, after forty months in office, as a result of corruption and financial scandal. Kubar was succeeded by Mohammed Bin Othman, who tried to restore public confidence in government and to seek harmonious relationships between his government and leadership with their interests on the one hand, and between the government and the Royal Diwan on the other.[57]

Bin Othman's cabinet survived until 1963, when it was replaced by Muhiaddin Fekini's cabinet, whose constitutional changes transformed the country from a federal to a unitary form of government. Fekini was faced with public demands to renegotiate the British-American-Libyan treaties. Clashes between demonstrating students and the powerful Cyrenaica Defense Force (CDF) in Benghazi brought to a head the issue of cabinet authority versus the authority of the Royal Diwan over the CDF in particular, and the police force in general, forcing Fekini to resign.[58]

The liberally educated and progressive Fekini was replaced by the conservative Muntasir (his second term), who stressed stability based on discipline and public order. Poor health was Muntasir's valid reason for resigning in 1965, when he was named head of the Royal Diwan. Husayn Maziq was appointed Muntasir's successor. Maziq had had a long career in government service and had served as foreign minister under Muntasir. Even though his education was very limited, he proved to be intelligent and hardworking.

Maziq met with violent demonstrations from the public and sharp attacks from the opposition over two issues: Libyan failure to assist its Arab brethren in the 1967 Arab-Israeli War and his decision to resume oil shipments to Western Europe. He was forced to resign on July 1, 1967.[59]

Abdulgader al-Badria was named prime minister and served for only five months, to be replaced by Abdulhamid al-Bakkush, a thirty-five-year old lawyer. Bakkush tried to balance his cabinet with conservative-liberal members, to appeal to the newly powerful young educated groups, and at the same time to keep peaceful relationships with the Royal Diwan and the old traditional leaders. But he was faced with accusations of corruption and favoritism. His governing approach antagonized the older generation and their leaders, and he was tolerated for only eleven months.[60] At the end of 1968, Bakkush was replaced by Wanis al-Gaddafi, a veteran of many previous cabinets. His main interest was the implementation of administrative reform, but the short period of time he spent in office before the Revolution of September 1969, did not allow his plans to unfold.[61]

In total, during this period of seventeen years, there were eleven cabinets (averaging eighteen months per cabinet), with thirty-two reshuffles (averaging six months each) and a total of 101 cabinet members in office. If the cabinet members appointed more than once were counted for each appointment, the total comes to 141 ministers. The ministers rarely had time to familiarize themselves with the issues of their posts, or to develop future plans and strategy for their departments. They were always under the threat of being dismissed or switched. Most of them were there to get for themselves everything they could in the shortest period possible.

As far as quality is concerned, the great majority of these cabinet members were incapable of handling the fundamental issues of their posts. They were chosen either to balance regional interests, or for their past and present support to the king. They were also chosen not for qualifications and skills, or political ideology and experience, but for the family, tribal, and religious influence they represented. These elements declined in number in the second half of this period with the rise of technocrats and bureaucrats in power.[62]

The premiership was dominated by traditionally powerful families or tribal members. Out of eleven prime ministers, seven were influential tribal leaders, three were members of influential families, three were university graduates, two had moderate administrative experience, and all but one had supported the Senussi family or demonstrated loyalty to the king himself prior to their appointment.

With universal public pressure, tremendous socioeconomic changes in Libya, and exigencies arising from the regional and international environments, the government was forced to attempt more changes than it could control or administer. The political and administrative scene in the country deteriorated, and the last days of the monarchical regime were marked by corruption, nepotism, maladministration, and fiscal dishonesty.[63]

The cabinet was controlled by the king, through his control of the prime minister. The frequent shuffling of officeholders promoted ministerial instability and effectively prevented individuals from consolidating their influence.[64] The Parliament was also controlled by the king through the control of the election by the cabinet. In the seven elections held in Libya (1952, 1955, 1960, 1964, 1965, 1967, and 1968), the government exercised substantial control in certification of candidates and results. This was mainly to secure the success of government candidates.[65] The tribal and parochial nature of Libyan society fostered voting on grounds of personality or on family or tribal connections, rather than on national issues or even local issues.[66] These voting criteria lost some of their strength within the urban centers, mainly Tripoli and Benghazi, where some of the candidates have run on issues and built an opposition.

Bureaucracy was another problem of the Libyan political system in the period from 1952 to 1969 and still is. It represented only regional and group interests and was a prototype of maladministration. Before the adoption of a unitary form of government, Libya had been ruled by four governments. In addition to the federal government which moved between three capitals, there were three provincial governments with an average of eight ministers each, and Tripolitania and Cyrenaica each employed more civil servants than the federal government. Each province followed its own policies without regard to the national federal policies—an extravagant, cumbersome, and inefficient arrangement, unmatched in similar conditions anywhere.[67]

After the unitary form was established, the number of government employees actually increased to 12 percent of the labor force, the highest number of government employees in the world. Civil service positions were used by the Parliament, Royal Diwan, cabinets, and senior officials as payoffs to their constituency and supporters, or to improve the well-being of their families or tribes.

Summary

Libya was a prototype of a poor state; it is still a prototype of a transitional one. For a long time the social structure of its society worked as a negative factor against change. All the variables which contribute to the shaping of the individual's attitudes, values, and behavior are of traditional origin. Furthermore, the main factor in the success of socioeconomic development programs and in building a modern national state, namely, mass participation and involvement, was absent. With economic change and accompanying exposure to new ideas, the country started its real movement on the path of development, at least of economic technological modernization. The economic change was accompanied by deep imbalances in the society, its economic sectors, and its political system. The social environment, traditions, and customs matched neither the new economic conditions nor the new political arrangement. Political leadership deterred the public from real involvement in the affairs of their society.

Government was a remote affair over which one urban voter had little, if any, control. The country folk, represented in the national and provincial assemblies and departments by their traditional leaders, neither expected to control nor felt the need to do so. Election offered a choice only of candidates with fixed ascriptive requirements rather than of programs.[68] Jobs were distributed on the bases of kinship and loyalty. Government offices were inaccessible, for the majority of public and government services were handled as favors to the recipients. The king, his prime ministers, and his advisers, lacked either the ability or the will to introduce innovations into the political structure to bring that structure into balance with the socioeconomic modernization in the region. In short, they failed to bridge the gap between socioeconomic change and political development. They failed to absorb the new modernizing groups into the political system, and ignored the new demands and expectations. Instead, the monarchy was static and worked against the system, and inflated opposition blocs by preventing the new groups from becoming involved in the governing process. The alienated young educated groups found themselves excluded from the system. D. Lerner commented, "They are dressed up with nowhere to go."[69] In one of his very few speeches, King Idris acknowledged, "The wealth [of Libya] God has given us from our soil," and warned, "The struggle ahead will not be less strenuous than during the past ten years. Prosperity has its own problems."[70] His assessment and forecast were accurate, although he never utilized them.

In short, the social structure of the Libyan society, its economic resources, changes in its economy, and the historical background of the region and its inhabitants afford the basis requisite to understanding Libyan society and politics. In particular, historical events and the socioeconomic and political environments in Libya have suggested that public political participation might be of great importance for the political and socioeconomic development processes and also might contribute to the development and stability of the state.

Notes

1. Richard F. Nyrop, et al., *Area Handbook for Libya* (Washington, D.C.: U.S. Government Printing Office, 1973).

2. Monte Palmer, *The Dilemmas of Political Development: An Introduction to the Politics of the Developing Areas* (Itasca, Ill.: F. W. Peacock Publishers, 1973).

3. Salaheddin S. Hassan, "The Genesis of the Political Leadership of Libya,

SOCIAL, ECONOMIC, AND HISTORICAL MILIEUS

1952-1969: Historical Origins and Development of Its Component Elements" (Ph.D. diss., The George Washington University, June 1970).

4. Ibid., p. 192. In his valuable study, Salaheddin Hassan succeeded in tracing origins and backgrounds of the families which practically ran Libya during eighteen years of monarchy.

5. Ibid., p. 49.

6. N. Ziyada, *Libya* (Beirut: The American University Press, 1948), p. 12, quoted in Hassan, "The Genesis of Leadership," p. 91.

7. *Shulat al Hurriyya* (Tripoli), 11 February 1951, quoted in Salaheddin Hassan, "The Genesis of Political Leadership," p. 91.

8. Nyrop, *Area Handbook*, p. 115.

9. The International Bank for Reconstruction and Development, *The Economic Development* of Libya (Baltimore: The Johns Hopkins University Press, 1960), p. 8.

10. Nyrop, *Area Handbook*, p. 116.

11. Ministry of Planning, LAR, *The Development of Education in Libyan Arab Republic* (Tripoli: Government Press, April 1973), p. 44.

12. Nyrop, *Area Handbook,* p. 5.

13. Ibid., p. 117.

14. Ministry of Planning *Development of Education in Libyan Arab Republic,* vol. 8 (Tripoli: Government Press, April 1, 1973), pp. 12-42; 115-18.

15. Ibid., p. 9.

16. C. L. Taylor, and M. C. Hudson, *World Handbook of Politics and Social Indicators,* 2nd ed.(New Haven: Yale University Press, 1972), p. 202.

17. Nyrop, *Area Handbook*, p. 57.

18. Ibid.

19. Benjamin Higgins, *Economic Development: Problems Principles, and Policies,* rev. ed. (New York: W. W. Norton, 1962), p. 819.

20. Nyrop, *Area Handbook,* p. 3.

21. Benjamin Higgins, *Economic Development: Principles, Problems and Policies* (New York: W. W. Norton, 1959), p. 26.

22. William Zartment, ed., *Man, State, and Society in the Contemporary Maghrib.* (New York: Praeger Publishers, 1972), p. 345.

23. Elizabeth R. Hayford, "The Politics of the Kingdom of Libya in Historical Perspective" (Ph.D. diss., Tufts University, 1970), p. 457.

24. R. El-Mallakh, "The Economics of Rapid Growth: Libya," *Middle East Journal* (Summer 1969): 308.

25. See John Wright, *Libya* (New York: Praeger Publishers, 1969), pp. 257-58; Higgins, *Economic Development,* p. 822; Hayford, "Politics of the Kingdom of Libya," p. 435.

26. Ali A. Attiga, "The Economic Impact of Oil on Libyan Agriculture" in J. A. Allan, K. S. Mclachlan, and E. T. Penrose, eds., *Libya: Agriculture*

and Economic Development (London: Frank Cass, 1973), pp. 9-18.

27. Ministry of Planning, LAR, *National Accounts, 1962-1972* (Tripoli: Government Press, 1973).

28. Ruth First, *Libya: The Elusive Revolution* (Baltimore: Penquin Books, 1974), p. 145.

29. H. Mahdavy, "The Patterns and Problems of Economic Development in Rentier States: The Case of Iran" in M. A. Cook, *Studies in the Economic History of the Middle East from the Rise of Islam to the Present Day* (London: Oxford Press, 1970), pp. 428-467.

30. Wright, *Libya*, p. 259.

31. Robert Mabro, "La Libye, Un Etat Rentier?" in *Project 39*, quoted in First, *Libya*, pp. 149-150.

32. Ministry of Petroleum, LAR, *Libyan Oil* (Tripoli: Government Press, 1972), p. 215.

33. Higgins, *Economic Development*, p. 822.

34. *First,* Libya, p. 152.

35. Ibid., pp. 153-54, and Nyrop, *Area Handbook,* pp. 200-204.

36. First, *Libya,* p. 155.

37. Nyrop, *Area Handbook,* p. 203.

38. Ibid., pp. 203-204. See also, *El-Fajer El-Jadeed* (Tripoli), 3, 4, and 14 February 1975; Ministry of Planning, LAR, *The Three Year Plan for Economic and Social Development* (Tripoli: Government Press, 1974), pp. 175-202.

39. First, *Libya,* p. 171.

40. *El-Fajer El-Jadeed* (Tripoli), 6, 7 April; 31 December 1974. See also *Mediterranean News* (Malta), 9 June 1974, p. 8; Ministry of Planning, LAR, *The Three Year Plan,* pp. 204-223; and Ministry of Information, LAR, *First of September Revolution, Fifth Anniversary* (Tripoli: Government Press, 1975), pp. 67-83.

41. First, *Libya,* p. 162.

42. House of Commons Debates, January 8, 1942, vol. 377, cols. 77-78, quoted in M. Khadduri, *Modern Libya: A Study in Political Development* (Baltimore: Johns Hopkins University Press, 1963), p. 35.

43. Ibid., pp. 57-58. See also, *Jaridat Benghazi* (Benghazi), 7 August 1945, where al-Kikhya's letter was supported and considered a representation of Cyrenaican's opinion.

44. Khadduri, *Modern Libya,* p. 58.

45. Ibid., pp. 92-94.

46. Ibid., p. 129.

47. *New York Times,* 19 May 1949; Khadduri, *Modern Libya*, p. 132.

48. See Articles 2, 3, and 36-39 of the Libyan Constitution.

49. See chapters 5 and 6 of the Constitution. See also Khadduri, *Modern Libya,* appendix B and Hayford, "Politics of the Kingdom," pp. 220-223.

50. Hayford, "Politics of the Kingdom", p. 226.

51. Ibid., p. 227.

52. Henry Serrano Villard, *Libya: The New Arab Kingdom of North Africa* (Ithaca, N.Y.: Cornell University Press, 1956), p. 42.

53. First, *Libya,* p. 151.

54. Mohammed H. Heikal, *The Road to Ramadan* (London: W. Collins Sons, 1957), pp. 68-69.

55. Khadduri, *Modern Libya,* pp. 237-238; Hayford, "Politics of the Kingdom," pp. 248-249, *Time* (London) 6 February 1954, and Hasan, "Genesis of Leadership," p. xv.

56. Khadduri, *Modern Libya,* pp. 240-243; Hayford, "Politics of the Kingdom," p. 440.

57. Khadduri, "Genesis of Political Leadership," pp. 286-290, 298-312, 314-317; Hayford, "Politics of the Kingdom," pp. 253-58; Wright, *Libya,* pp. 237-242.

58. Hayford, "Politics of the Kingdom," p. 259; *Christian Science Monitor* (January 27, 1964), *Maghreb Digest* (February, 1964), p. 14.

59. Hayford, "Politics of the Kingdom," p. 262; *New York Times* (March 22, 1965); *African Diary* 7 (August 6-12, 1967), p. 515.

60. *Christian Science Monitor* (April 29, 1968); Hassan "Genesis of Leadership," pp. 447-48; Hayford, "The Politics of the Kingdom", pp. 265-66.

61. Hasan, "Genesis of Leadership," pp. 440, 448, xv.

62. Ibid., p. 448.

63. An example of corruption is "the occidental oil concessions" case where two Libyan ministers became involved in bribery and disclosure of cabinet secrets. See *Wall Street Journal* (8 February 1973); see also Leonard Mosley, *Power Play: Oil in the Middle East* (New York: Random House, 1973), pp. 328-333.

64. First, *Libya,* p. 78.

65. Nyrop, *Area Handbook,* p. 159.

66. See Lewis and Gordon, "Libya After Two Years of Independence," *Middle East Journal* 8, no. 1 (Winter 1954), pp. 41-53; Lewis, "Libya: An Experience," *Current History* (August 1955), pp. 102-109; and Hayford, "Politics of the Kingdom," p. 235.

67. Wright, *Libya,* p. 260.

68. Ibid., p. 241.

69. See Lerner, *The Passing of Traditional Society: Modernizing the Middle East* (Glencoe, Ill.: Free Press, 1958).

70. On the occasion of the Tenth Anniversary of Independence, 24 December 1961, quoted in Wright, *Libya,* p. 259.

3

The Impact of Sociopolitical Change on Economic Development in Libya
Omar I. El Fathaly and *Fathi S. Abusedra*

Models and plans suggested to or *imposed* on the developing world have found little, if any, applicability as prescriptive formulas for the transformation of those nations. Such outside proposals have contained, as a fundamental proposition, certain conditions of political and economic development, many of which do not exist in the developing world. As Rustow convincingly maintained,

> there is no reason to search for a single universal recipe ... Instead each country must start with frank assessment of its particular liabilities and assets, and each will be able to learn most from those countries whose problems closely resemble its own.[1]

The present study provides evidence supporting the premises that (a) the specific sociopolitical environment in Libya influences the developmental operation of its policy and (b) fundamental changes in the traditional organizations and structure of society are essential for the achievement of rapid successful sociopolitical and economic development.

Socioeconomic History

At the time independence was achieved, in 1951, Libya was one of the poorest nations in the world. B. Higgins wrote:

> Libya's great merit as a case study is [that it is] a prototype of [a] poor country. ... We need not construct abstract models of an economy where the bulk of the people live on a subsistence level, where there are no sources of power and no mineral resources, where agricultural expansion is severely limited by climatic conditions, where capital formation is zero or less, where there is no skilled labor supply and no indigenous entrepreneurship. When Libya became an independent kingdom under U.N. auspices (December '51), it fulfilled all these conditions. Libya is at the bottom of the range in income and resources and so provides a reference point for comparison with other countries.[2]

Libyan society was faced with a multiplicity of ethnic, tribal, and regional conflicts; deeply embedded problems of poverty, ignorance, and disease; religious and cultural confusion; and the crushing effects of merciless political occupation and natural calamity. For Libyan society (indeed, for the whole Arab world), the dilemma of the masses has constituted the deepest and most challenging problem of government.[3]

Religious, tribal, and family elements constituted a very important part of the political leadership up to late 1969. These elements gained importance from the significant societal role they have played and the interest of the top leadership in ruling the country along such (religious, tribal, and family) lines.[4]

Conflicts among regional interests and over the legal authorities of boundaries have resulted in government instability. Libya was ruled by four governments, three provincials and one federal or national, and the national government maintained three capitals, periodically moving from one to the other. Twelve percent of the labor force, an extravagant, burdensome, and inefficient number, was under government employment. Bureaucracy was controlled by ascriptive leadership, aging rules, and obsolete procedures; moreover, it was protected by strong police organizations. This situation created a society of masses and lords, as well as inaccessible government offices which inflated the gap between the government and the citizens.

The bleak picture changed with the first major oil discovery in 1959, and the rapid development of this new resource. Within only eight years of the first shipment, Libya became the world's fourth largest exporter of crude oil. The rate at which Libyan crude oil production and exports rose during the sixties, seventeenfold over the period from 1962 to 1969, was unprecedented anywhere else in the world.[5] Thus, "Libya has moved. . . . from the status of capital deficit to a capital surplus nation,..."[6]

Table 3-1 dramatizes the rapid increases in oil production and revenues during the sixties. Libya's suddenly augmented fiscal dependence on oil resources is reflected in the increasing ratio of oil revenues to total revenues. There is no doubt that the drastic rise in oil prices after October 1973 will be reflected in higher oil revenues for the Libyan government in 1974 and years to come. These data underscore the leading role assumed by Libya in demanding higher prices, upgraded government "take," and a more participatory function for exporting countries in oil activities and price determination, which together have changed the economic structure of the international oil industry.

Since oil revenues accrue directly to the government and are its main source of wealth, the future development of the nation depends primarily on the management and allocation of oil revenues. Therefore, the government's regular and developmental budget expenditures are by far the most significant factors in the economy as is shown in Table 3-2.

Despite the fact that economic planning started in Libya with independence, through the uncoordinated international aid programs, the first comprehensive economic and social development plan did not take shape until 1963. This was partly due to the regional rather than national commitment of the leaders and conflicting advice given to the government until several institutional changes

Table 3-1
Oil Production and the Contribution of Oil Revenue to Total Revenue

Year	Oil Production (in millions of metric tons)	Total Revenues (in millions U.S. dollars)	Oil Revenues Million U.S. dollars	Oil Revenues Percentage of Total Revenue
1962	8.7	86,698	6,720	7.8
1963	21.8	121,050	24,192	20.0
1964	40.7	212,918	79,968	37.6
1965	57.5	289,027	183,120	63.6
1966	71.9	423,360	280,277	66.6
1967	82.1	7080,912	907,481	83.4
1968	122.8	838,320	641,807	76.5
1969	146.3	1205,904	933,371	77.4
1970	156.2	1491,840	1221,306	82.0
1971	136.8	1853,177	1574,969	84.9
1972	109.2	2840,076	2191,788	88.4
1973	107.9	2459,772	2098,572	85.3
1974	74.04	8619,240	8214,870	95.3
1975	72.02	6999,290	6723,360	95.1
1976	94.31	Not Available	Not Available	Not Available

Source: For Production: (1) *Libyan Oil*, Ministry of Petroleum, Tripoli, Libya, 1972, p. 22. (2) *International Petroleum Encyclopedia*, New York, 1974, p. 306. (3) Annual Report, Ministry of Petroleum Tripoli, Libya, vol. 74-76; For Revenues: (1) Fourteenth Annual Report: Bank of Libya, Tripoli, Libya, 1970, p. 116. (2) Seventeenth Annual Report: Bank of Libya, Tripoli, Libya, 1973, p. 110. (3) Twentieth Annual Report: Bank of Libya, Tripoli, Libya, 1976, pp. 114-116. (4) Journal of Arab Oil, vol. 10, July 1975, p. 7.

were adopted. The most important changes were the replacement of the federal governmental system by a unitary form in order to facilitate greater administrative control as well as the concentration of planning authorities into one body, namely the Ministry of Planning.

The plan, covering the period from 1963 to 1968, allocated Libyan dinar (L.D.) 169 Million, but this was later raised to a total of L.D. 363 Million. Infrastructure projects were emphasized, including electric power, transportation, and public works. Infrastructure projects absorbed about 43 percent of the total allocations. At the time, allocations for agriculture, education, industry, health, and housing sectors were 10, 9, 5, 4, and 11 percent of the total, respectively. In 1968 the plan was extended through the fiscal year 1968-1969 (April to March) to permit a thorough preparation of a second plan and to complete the unfinished projects scheduled in the first.[7]

The development process in the sixties was accompanied by several bottlenecks and shortcomings. A lack of balanced growth among the different sectors of the national economy led to a complete change of the economy's structure with hypertrophy of the oil sector at the expense of other producing sectors. Failure to utilize the large demand for goods and services, created by the oil

Table 3-2
Ordinary and Development Budgets from 1963-1964 to 1976-1977

Fiscal Year	Ordinary Budget (in million U.S. dollars)	Development Budget (in million U.S. dollars)
1963-1964	168.672	42.000
1964-1965	215.712	77.280
1965-1966	278.880	176.164
1966-1967	378.336	276.528
1967-1968	571.200	309.120
1968-1969	745.920	413.280
1969-1970	639.408	487.200
1970-1971	614.208	672.000
1971-1972	676.704	1013.376
1972-1973	853.440	1334.928
1973-1974	1041.264	2486.400
1974-1975	1469.388	3780.000
1975-1976	1680.000	4317.600
1976-1977	1958.880	5107.200

Source: (1) Ministry of Petroleum, *Libyan Oil* (Tripoli, 1972), p. 125. (2) Eighteenth Annual Report: Bank of Libya, Tripoli, Libya, 1973-1974, pp. 165, 167. (3) Twentieth Annual Report: Bank of Libya, Tripoli, Libya, 1975, pp. 94, 100. (4) *Algehad Newspaper*, 29/12/76, p. 2. (5) Fifth Annual Report, Editing department, 1972-1973, pp. 23, 146.

activity for the development of a local production, amounted to economic negligence. Without such development other sectors could not cope with the high productivity in the oil sector, and there resulted a heavy reliance on imports, which increased over threefold during the sixties.[8] The term *rentier* state, elucidated by R. Mabro and H. Mahdavy, found felicitous application to Libya at this time. In this context, rentier state refers to a state that receives large revenues from its raw material production and exportation, where this process has very little to do with its domestic economic growth because other production is very insignificant.[9] Inequitable regional development led to widespread migration of individuals from the neglected rural villages and remote areas to urban centers. There was substantial disparity in the distribution of individual income. Moreover, inflation was rising with deteriorating social and economic effects. The adoption of large-scale programs costing vast amounts of money put considerable pressure on the administration and the small labor force.

The First of September Revolution (1969) changed the priorities of the development strategy by giving different emphasis to certain sectors. Ever since the start of the new regime, attention has been focused on planning and development to effectuate a shift in the social and economic structures from a state of full dependence on the oil sector to one of balanced growth for all the sectors. A sum of $680,000,000 was allocated to the development budget of 1970-1971, $1,025,440,000 was thus allotted for 1971-1972, and $1,505,860,000 for 1972-1973; these allocations were ad hoc investment programs pending the establishment of institutional frameworks and priorities.

In June 1972 the government announced a three-year development plan (for 1973-1975). The plan's allocations among sectors are listed in Table 3-3. In September 1974, total allocations were raised to $7,327,000,000, an increase of about $582,000,000. In February 1975, allocations were raised again to bring the total to $8,741,400,000.[10]

These allocations show the change in priorities of the government. Allocations for the agriculture sector represent over 16 percent of the total while those for the industry sector (excluding mining) represent over 11 percent of the total. In addition, these two sectors would benefit the most from developing the transportation, electricity, and housing sectors (totaling 2,949.05 million dollars).

The plan has aimed at achieving a maximum growth rate in real GNP accompanied by greater diversification in the structure of the economy. A deliberate effort has been made to lessen the dependence on the oil sector. By applying conservation measures, reasonable rates of crude oil extraction were to be maintained in order to prolong the life of oil resources.[11] A new five-year plan for (1976-1980) was introduced and these allocations amounted to 24.234 billion dollars aimed at an annual increase of 10.5 percent in GNP and 26 percent in industrial production.

Table 3-3
Allocations Among Sectors in the 1973-1975 Plan

Sector	Allocations (in million U.S. dollars)	Percentage of Total
Housing	1213.968	18.4
Agriculture	1101.408	16.6
Electricity and water	864.864	13.1
Transport and communication	853.768	12.9
Industry	778.176	11.8
Education	645.456	9.8
Public services	627.312	9.5
Health	238.560	3.6
Petroleum	164.304	2.5
Construction	20.832	0.3
Other minerals	9.744	0.2
Bank and insurance	1.344	–
Reserves	80.304	1.2
Total	6602.400	100.0

Source: *The Three Years Plan* (1972-1975), Ministry of Planning, Libya, p. 90.

Much in line with the previous plan, the new plan is targeted at achieving diversification of the national economy by improving the economy's infrastructure projects and agricultural and industrial development.

The division of total allocations among the different sectors is given in Table 3-4. Allocations for agriculture amounted to 17.5 percent, while those earmarked for industry represented 15.3 percent. These numbers reflect the emphasis given to the two sectors.

Realizing that oil resources are depletable and alternative sources of revenues should be developed quickly, the new regime has implemented a strategy to set up an effective economic infrastructure on which an "oil-less" future could be based. This is clearly in the oil conservation measures and in the apparent emphasis of the development plan upon the agricultural and industrial sectors.

Libya currently has an abundant supply of capital, a situation which has inspired some economists to suggest a model for "development with an unlimited supply of capital,"[12] as an alternative to the more common model which

Table 3-4
Five-Year Development Plan Allocations by Sector (*U.S. Million Dollars*)

Development Sector	Total Expenditure (1976-1980)
Agriculture and agrarian reform	1496.195
Integral agricultural development	2625.168
Nutrition and marine wealth	138.939
Industry and mineral wealth	3661.570
Oil and gas exploration	2177.939
Electricity	1826.647
Education	1580.645
Information and Culture	306.902
Manpower	140.445
Public Health	575.921
Social Affairs and social security	145.008
Housing	2668.633
Security services	117.600
Municipalities	1855.170
Transport and communications	2123.970
Marine transport	1254.960
Planning and scientific research	190.663
Trade and marketing	109.973
Reserve	1093.119
Total	24091.200

Source: *Middle East Economic Digest* 20 (January 30, 1976) (5): 22.

describes "development with unlimited supply of labor."[13] However, development also requires a change in the social and political environment.[14]

Recognizing the effects of sociopolitical structure on economic development in particular and overall development in general, the leadership of the revolutionary regime, in order to avert deficiencies of the old regime's policies, followed a number of methods designed to subvert the old traditional leadership and institutions and substitute new ones. These methods, which were to facilitate the building of a new society and the creation of a favorable environment for socioeconomic and political development, included psychological, geographical, and political schemes.

An intense public doubt concerning the ability of the traditional leadership to control, govern, or change arose. These leaders represented an ascriptive type of leadership (selected on the basis of inheritance, traditional reputation, socioeconomic status, religiousness, and age) whose sociopolitical and economic institutions were unable to regulate the polity and the whole of society.

The revolutionary leadership also identified the traditional leadership with the old regime and its politically and economically corrupt system, thereby relating all the negative aspects of the old regime to those leaders. In addition, the traditional leadership was identified with the colonial powers which had formerly controlled the country. In an attempt to divorce the traditional leadership from its ground of support in the community, these leaders were accused of "wrongdoing" against "public interest."

The psychological method was designed to break the congruency between the public and its traditional leaders and institutions, to draw public attention to a different type of leadership (the modernizers) which more or less represented the new national and local leadership, and to destroy public trust in and loyalty to traditional leaders. With this accomplished it would be possible to build new bridges between the public and the modernizing leadership.

By the use of what was called the "cross-lines" geographical approach, localities were divided into zones (sections) crossing old tribal boundaries, combining parts of different tribes within one zone, in an effort to destroy the power of traditional institutions and regional or local kinship. This zoning served to destroy traditional regional identity along with its political and social power, and to relocate the traditional administrative power centers. Figures 3-1 and 3-2 illustrate the main concepts of this approach.

The geographical method was more effective when it was followed by a number of supportive actions. By government code the title of "sheikh" was changed to zone administrator, and the old ascriptive prerequisites for leadership were replaced by education, knowledge, and ability, as determined by oral and written examinations. The revolutionary leadership also required that all community affairs (religious, social, and economic), which were formerly handled largely by the sheikhs, be referred to government administration.

The geographical method, combined with supportive legal actions, aimed to

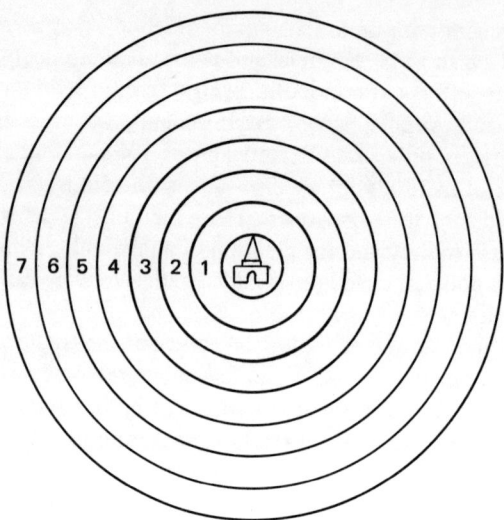

Note: The former system, where geographical boundaries of tribes are schematically represented as closed concentric circles around a local administration, where a tribe is represented in the administration according to its degree of influence and dominance.

Figure 3-1. Tribalization of Administrative Boundaries

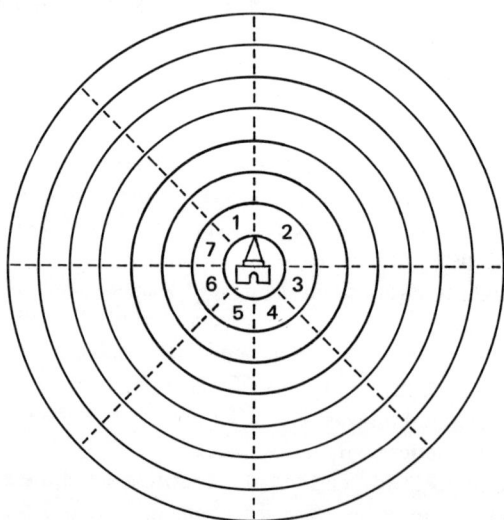

Note: Schematic diagram of the new system, showing the geographical boundaries of sections or zones which cross old tribal boundaries and connect each zone with the local administration, where each zone (and not tribe) is represented in the local government by its zone administrator.

Figure 3-2. Detribalization of Administrative Boundaries

shake the superior status of the old sheikhs and their families as a source of power and the closed circle of the tribal system. It also introduced individuals of a traditional society to modern governmental institutions which would replace the old traditional organizations and units. In this way a link was created between society and government.

Neither the psychological nor the geographical methods would produce the requisite changes and results unless accompanied by political strategies. One such approach involved bridging the gap left by the abolition of the tribal system through the integration of the mass into a one-party system. The resulting Arab Socialist Union (ASU) was designed to encourage the masses to participate in the establishment of local policies and in other community affairs through the party units and structure. Modeled after the Egyptian forerunner, the ASU was directed to create a "popular alliance of the working force," meaning peasants, nonagricultural working people, soldiers, the revolutionary intelligentsia, and "nonexploiting national capitalists."[15]

The political leadership looked to the party as the political institution through which the public could participate and be motivated, mobilized, and politicized at the same time. The single organization was to reflect government interests and goals on the one hand while remaining sensitive to public demands and aspirations on the other. Finally, the ASU would function as a source of organized support to the leadership and its strategies whenever a display of such support was needed.

The creation of the ASU resulted, as expected, in a virtual war between the party organizers and the bureaucrats, who were supported in many cases by the traditional leadership elements within and without the bureaucracy. The bureaucracy was accused of being the main obstacle in the way of development and creating trivial technical issues to sabotage the revolutionary regime programs.

The conflict of power and interests between a premature political organization and relatively skillful bureaucrats crippled the organization and forced the political leadership to adopt a second political method, "the popular revolution," aimed at the following: (1) destroying the classical bureaucratic system, by giving the public the whole power and authority to change, dismiss, and elect public officials on all levels with the exception of the Revolutionary Command Council (RCC) officers, cabinet members, and military and police personnel; (2) giving the public a free hand in changing, omitting, or issuing new laws and regulations to suit the new revolutionary era and programs, thereby removing all the legal and administrative obstacles in the way of revolutionary change; (3) mobilizing the public behind the leaders when the ASU at that stage had failed to do so, and (4) destroying the old traditional sociopolitical power structure by creating a new type of community leadership based on loyalty to the regime, ability, and knowledge.

The popular revolution approach was founded on the assumption that the public is the most important variable in the development process, and "the changes that matter are in the way people live, work, think, and hope. . . . This is where the policy makers must begin."[16] Bringing the public to more supportive attitudes and roles would significantly contribute to the success of development plans. Therefore, public participation and involvement was given priority. Needs and expectations of the public could be met more effectively through its participation within the framework of modern institutions. Such involvement has, in part, taken the form of elected committees (popular committees) that run the communities, public offices, and public organizations and institutes. This approach has found immediate success in the creation of a sense of civic responsibility and the shift of public orientation and values away from the influence of traditionalism.

Conclusion

Changes in the sociopolitical structure of Libya are necessary for the success of economic change and overall development. Like other developing countries, Libya has had a number of traditions, customs, and institutions which have stood in the way of such growth, and these will have to be changed if a rapid rate of development is to be achieved.[17]

The revolutionary regime realized that new leadership and new modern institutions would be essential in providing the environment that favored the success of its revolution. Since traditional leadership lacked the orientation, background, attitudes, values, or interests which would make them able or willing to implement revolutionary changes and policies, these leaders were stripped of their power and replaced by younger, better educated people who shared the values and commitments of the revolutionary leadership.

It has been hoped that the modernizing leaders, having fewer obligations to their immediate constituencies, would be better able to change the focus of planning from the regional or local to the national interest level. The process of development will be geared more to scientific and appropriate methods. The commitment to regional, local, or specific group interests will disappear. A healthy environment for overall development which allows accurate assessments of the national needs and resources requires disengagement from commitment to specific group interests as well as the application of appropriate scientific methods.

The dismantling of the traditional institutions (clan, tribe, family, and religion) or minimization of their power and influence would bring the public into direct contact and better communication with the government and its modern political institutions. Eventually, this contact would occasion government facilities and programs that would be more suitably geared to public needs and interests.

Therefore, the traditional leadership and institutions, and their components and limited abilities, have been considered as part of the past, inapplicable to the planning and execution of the development process in a modern framework. At the same time, the authors recognize that sociopolitical institutions are basic prerequisites for economic development, even more basic than economic historians have prescribed. Building new noneconomic institutions, as Eisenstadt and others suggested, is vitally important for the "productivization and modernization of traditional elements," and will eventually lead to the politicization of the society.[18] The institutionalization of Libyan society, in a modern sense of the term, would enable the masses to make decisions and develop policies that reflect the society's aspirations and needs within the bounds of a realistic assessment of resources and priorities. Institutionalization would also help the society deal with the problems created by change and modernization more adequately.

These fundamental changes in the Libyan sociopolitical structure, even with some inevitable defects, were expected to succeed in eliminating many obstacles impeding development. These have provided conditions of an environment favorable to development without which the revolutionary economic programs cannot be successfully implemented.

It may be concluded that prospects of rapid economic growth and development are gloomy. Traditional institutions, social structure, attitudes, values, and methods pose an obstinate barrier to those seeking the changes that are imperative for such growth. The actual results of these changes will provide us with more than speculative exercise in the future.

Notes

1. D. Rustow, *A World of Nations: Problems of Political Modernization* (Washington, D.C.: The Brookings Institution, 1967), pp. 275-276.

2. Benjamin Higgins, *Economic Development* (New York: W. W. Norton, 1959), rev. ed., p. 26.

3. For analysis of political social psychology of the Arab mind, see E. Salem in *Readings in Arab Middle Eastern Societies and Cultures*, edited by A. Lutfiyya and C. Churchill (The Hague: Mouton and Co., 1970), pp. 402-411.

4. For a discussion of leadership see Salaheddin S. Hassan "The Political Leadership of Libya 1952-1969" (Ph.D. diss. The George Washington University, 1973), chaps. 1, 2, 3.

5. Libyan Arab Republic, Ministry of Petroleum, *The Libyan Oil* (Tripoli, 1972).

6. Ragoei El Mallakh, "The Economics of Rapid Growth: Libya," *Middle East Journal* (Summer 1969), p. 308.

7. Kingdom of Libya, Ministry of Planning and Development, *Five Year Economic and Social Development Plan 1963-1968* (Tripoli, 1963).

8. Ministry of Planning, *National Accounts 1962-1972* (Tripoli, 1973).

9. See Robert Mabro, "La Libye, Un Etat Rentier?" in *Project 39*, November 1969; H. Mahdavy, "The Patterns and Problems of Economic Development in Rentier States: The Case of Iran," in M. A. Cook, *Studies in the Economic History of the Middle East from the Rise of Islam to the Present Day* (Oxford, 1970), pp. 428-467; and Ruth First, *Libya: The Elusive Revolution* (Baltimore: Penguin Books, 1974), pp. 145-148.

10. *Middle East Economic Digest*, vol. 19, no. 8 (February 21, 1975).

11. Ministry of Planning, Libyan Arab Republic, *Three Year Economic and Social Development Plan, 1973-1975* (Tripoli, 1973), chap. 2.

12. Higgins, *Economic Development*, chap. 35.

13. For a discussion of this model see: W. A. Lewis, *Economic Development with Unlimited Supplies of Labour* (The Manchester School, May 1954); and John Fei and Gustav Rainis, *Development of Labor Surplus Economy* (Homewood, Ill.: Richard D. Irwin, 1964).

14. Louis J. Walinsky, *The Planning and Execution of Economic Development* (New York: McGraw-Hill, 1963), p. 22.

15. Richard F. Myrop, et al., *Area Handbook for Libya* (Washington, D.C.: The American University, 1972), 2nd ed. pp. 170-175.

16. Max W. Thornburg, *People and Policy in the Middle East* (New York: W. W. Norton, 1964), p. 12.

17. International Bank for Reconstruction and Development, *The Economic Development of Libya* (Baltimore: Johns Hopkins University Press, 1960), p. 9.

18. See S. N. Eisenstadt, "Modernization and Conditions of Sustained Growth," *World Politics* 16 (July 1964); and Benjamin Rivlin and Joseph S. Szyliowicz, *The Contemporary Middle East: Tradition and Innovation* (New York: Random House, 1965), pp. 397-410 and 415-416.

Part II

4

Political Development Among Rural Libyans
Omar I. El Fathaly and Monte Palmer

According to most development theorists, no segment of society is less productive economically, less involved politically, and less receptive to governmental efforts to induce political, economic, and social change than the uneducated rural mass.

From the perspective of a Libyan regime with the stated goal of transforming Libya into a modern society in the shortest time possible, the presumed resistance of rural population to political and economic modernization presents a problem of enormous proportions, for Libya, in spite of its vast oil resources, remains a predominantly uneducated rural society.

This chapter has several objectives. The first is to place Libya's modernization efforts in theoretical perspective by contrasting the dominant structural and behavioral characteristics of ideal type traditional societies such as Libya so recently typified with the structural and behavioral characteristics of ideal type modern societies such as Libya would like to become. This step is essential for it provides some concept of the magnitude of the social transformation envisioned by the Libyan government and illustrates the complexities of the modernization process.

Our second objective is to examine the extent to which Libya's predominantly rural population is, in fact, as traditional as people generally assume. We feel this is an important question, for if rural Libyans do not conform to the traditional model they may prove to be far easier to integrate into a modern society than is generally anticipated. Knowledge of the traditionalness of Libya's rural population should also be of use to the revolutionary government in designing strategies to better facilitate the implementation and acceptance of their modernization programs among Libya's predominantly rural populations. If traditional Libyans are truly "tradition bound," for example, the government might seriously consider slowing its attempts to crush the established rural power structure and, instead, attempt to co-opt traditional leaders into the modernization process.

Our third and primary objective is to evaluate the political behavior of rural Libyans in reference to four indicators of political modernization: (1) preference for political leaders selected on the basis of achievement rather than the basis of ascription; (2) attitudinal predispositions to support administrative personnel; (3) an awareness and positive evaluation of efforts of the political system to improve the standard of life for all Libyans; and (4) participation in the political system and its agencies. In so doing we hope to provide some

---

This paper was originally presented at the 1977 Convention of the African Political Science Association, Rabat, Morocco.

indication of both the resistance of the rural Libyan population to political modernization and the extent to which the Libyan government has been successful in bridging the gap between the central government and Libya's predominantly rural mass.

Finally, our fourth objective is to compare the political behavior of rural Libyans with that of Libyans who live in less rural surroundings and who have experienced greater exposure both to education and the mass media. In making this comparison we hope to provide some measure of the political distance between rural and urban Libyans and to provide some indication of the political attitudes that might be forthcoming among the rural populations if the government's modernization programs are effective in radically transforming rural value structures. We realize, of course, that one cannot be certain that the behavior of rural Libyans, once altered, will approximate that of Libyans who currently live in less traditional surroundings. The comparisons will, however, provide more information than is currently available on the subject.

Methodology

Our analyses of the attitudes and behavior of rural Libyans is based upon the attitudinal survey of 10 percent of the adult male population of seven villages in the Libyan province of Zavia discussed in the introductory chapter.

Following an information model suggested by Daniel Lerner's *The Passing of Traditional Society*, the sample of 576 respondents was divided into traditional, transitional, and modern categories, based upon their level of education, urbanization, and media exposure.[1] Traditional or "rural" individuals for the purposes of the study are illiterate peasants and bedouins who lived in tribal villages far removed from the urban areas, who indicated that their exposure to television was virtually nill ($n = 211$).[2] Virtually all Libyans have experienced frequent exposure to the radio, with the rural population indicating a strong preference for religious and rural programs. The "modern" category consisted of individuals who had completed at least a secondary education (high school), who lived in quasi-urban areas, and who watched television on a regular basis ($n = 113$). A third category of individuals, the transitional, possessed a mixture of traditional and modern attributes ($n = 249$).

It is with the attitudes and behavior of the 211 individuals falling in the traditional or rural category that this chapter is concerned.

Some Theoretical Comparisons of Traditional and Modern Societies

Development theorists from the era of Tonnies and Weber through more recent analysts such as Parsons, Khal, Apter, Riggs, Inkeles, Lerner, Sutton, and Sjoberg, have dichotomized human society into antithetical ideal types: the traditional and the modern.[3] Falling between the two polar categories lies a broad, vaguely defined entity referred to as "transitional."

The antithetical nature of the traditional modern dichotomy permeates virtually all levels of social analysis. Traditional societies are predominantly rural; modern societies are predominantly urban. Traditional societies are predominantly illiterate. Modern societies, in addition to being literate, are characterized by near universal education. Communications in traditional societies are based upon oral, face-to-face contacts. Communications in modern societies are media intense.

The social structure of traditional societies is based upon the extended family and it is the extended family that bears primary responsibility for nurturing individuals into adulthood, shaping their basic values to conform with the needs of society, determining their occupations, selecting their spouses, defining their recreational groups (mainly relatives), caring for their welfare in time of illness or old age, providing their security from external enemies, and, as most extended families bear collective responsibility for the behavior of their members, rigidly policing their behavior to minimize inter-family conflict.

The social structure of modern societies is a highly differentiated network of specialized socioeconomic and political units which reach their apex in the state. It is the state and not the extended family that bears ultimate responsibility for meeting the individual's various needs, and it is the state that shapes the fundamental values of the individual.

Traditional societies are characterized by poorly differentiated, agrarian, family based, barter economies which neither utilize nor generate innovative technology and which seldom provide goods and services beyond the level of bare subsistence. Modern societies are characterized by highly differentiated, industrialized market or command economies dominated by "public" corporations which both utilize and generate innovative technology and which create a surplus of goods and services sufficient to provide most members of society with a standard of living well in excess of mere subsistence.

The political systems of traditional societies are similarly characterized by rudimentary organizational structures dominated by family-based tribal chieftains who justify their authority ascriptively on the basis of lineage, religion, or tradition and who, either individually or with the assistance of close relatives, perform both the input functions of interest articulation and interest aggregation (reading the masses) and the output functions of role making, rule making and rule adjudication. The political systems of modern societies are characterized by complex, highly differentiated organizational structures dominated by elites selected predominantly on the basis of achievement (merit). All political functions, including interest articulation, interest aggregation, rule making, rule administration, and rule adjudication, are by specialized units. Mass political participation in traditional societies is minimal; mass participation in modern societies is intense.

Finally, traditional cultures (religions, traditions, myths, norms, mores) justify established social, economic, and political patterns as the will of God or other supernatural forces and reinforce the operation and perpetuation of the traditional social order by stressing the values of passivity, fatalism, and conformity. Modern cultural systems justify established social, economic, and political patterns on the basis of supernatural appeals to God, dialectical materialism, or national destiny, but, in contrast to traditional cultures, stress political participation, achievement, creativity, nationalism, and other values essential to the operation and perpetuation of modern economic and political systems.

As human behavior tends to be profoundly shaped by the individual's structural and cultural milieu, it follows logically that the behavior patterns which tend to characterize traditional societies should also be antithetical to the behavior patterns which tend to characterize modern societies.

Traditional individuals, reflecting the values of traditional cultures, are said to be passive, fatalistic, conformist, and noninnovative. Modern individuals tend to have a far stronger sense of human volition; to be more aggressive, more innovative, and to be more imbued with what David McCelland has termed "achievement motivation." Moreover, because of their geographic isolation and general illiteracy, traditional individuals are said to be intensely superstitious or religious. Modern individuals, because of greater exposure to information, tend to be less religious.

Similarly, traditional individuals, reflecting the pervasive role of the extended family in the structuring of their lives and the shaping of their identity, are said to be particularistic and parochial. Kinship obligations ethically supersede moral obligations to any other group. Loyalty to the state, if awareness of the state exists at all, is minimal. Modern individuals, by contrast, are said to be universalistic. Kinship obligations are regularly superseded by occupational, political, and social obligations. Merit and the maximization of personal advantage outweigh kinship ties in the selection of employees and associates. The state rather than the family is the terminal focus of individual loyalty. Nationalism is pervasive.

As the ethical value hierarchy of traditional individuals places obligations to the family above obligations to other groups, conflict between families is intense and distrust of nonkinship groups tends to be pervasive. The breadth of political and economic networks in modern societies, by contrast, demands a broader, nonkinship foundation for interpersonal trust and interaction. In much the same manner, traditional individuals are said to be atomistic; to be concerned only with their own immediate needs and to have little concern for the needs of others. Modern individuals are said to manifest far greater recognition of a concern for the community as a whole.

As traditional behavior patterns are antithetical to behavior patterns characteristic of the world's more industrially developed societies, development theorists have generally hypothesized that traditional attitudes and behavior patterns serve as an obstacle to political and economic development.[4] It is assumed, for example, that the value structures of traditional individuals, and particularly their religiosity and tribalism, incline them to support ascriptive tribal elites rather than modernizing leaders. It is also assumed that individuals socialized to value the past will be predisposed to reject all programs of social and economic modernization regardless of their potential value to the individual and the community. In much the same manner, it is assumed that the fatalism and passivity of traditional individuals predispose them to shun getting involved in both public assistance programs designed to build regime support and political involvement programs designed to build links between modernizing leaders and the traditional masses.

The discussion presented in Chapter 2 indicates that Libya continues to manifest many of the structural attributes of a traditional society. The remainder of this chapter will examine the continued prevalence of traditional attitudes and behavior patterns among rural Libyans and their impact upon the political system.

Rural Libya as a Traditional Society

In terms of both development literature and the public statements of Libyan leaders, rural Libyans should manifest behavior that is intensely traditional. In particular, it should be characterized by tribalism, religiosity, particularism, fatalism, interpersonal distrust, and atomistic attitudes in reference to individuals beyond their circle of friends and relatives.

As a preliminary step in testing this hypothesis, questionnaire items relating to religiosity, particularlism, fatalism, interpersonal distrust, and atomism were factor analyzed to ascertain whether they actually represented discrete behavior patterns or whether they were merely all facets of singly underlying behavior dimension labeled traditionalism.[5] The factor analysis indicated that the five categories represented independent behavior dimensions. The items with the strongest loading in each cluster were then combined to form, respectively, a religiosity scale, a particularism scale, an atomism scale, an interpersonal distrust scale, and a fatalism scale. A single questionnaire item loaded on the atomism factor, thereby precluding the development of an atomism scale.

Religiosity

The religiosity scale consisted of two items, the percentage distributions for which appear in Table 4-1. Possible scores of the religiosity scale ranged from 2 through 10, with 2 representing the most religious response and 10 the least. Scores of 2, 3, or 4 were considered intensely religious; 5, religious; 6 and 7, moderately religious; and 8 through 10 minimally religious.

Stated in less formal terms, the intensely religious category of the religiosity scale consisted of individuals who prayed at the mosque every day and described themselves as being at least very religious or individuals who described themselves as being extremely religious and prayed at the mosque at least twice a week. The religious category included individuals who, at minimum, described themselves as being extremely religious and prayed at the mosque at least once a week or who described themselves as being somewhat religious and prayed everyday. The least religious category consisted of individuals who indicated they were not religious and prayed at the mosque once a year or less.

Aside from these divisions, if religiosity were defined as being somewhat religious and praying at the mosque at least once a week, all but 4 percent of the rural sample would have fallen in the religious category. The influence of religion in rural Libya is clearly pervasive. If religion is the cornerstone of

Table 4-1
Religiosity among Rural Libyans

	Percentage	
Are you a religious man?		(*n* = 209)
Extremely religious	13.4	
Very religious	52.6	
Somewhat religious	33.0	
Don't know	1.0	
	100.0	
How often do you pray in the mosque?		(*n* = 211)
Every day	26.5	
Twice a week	19.9	
Once a week	45.5	
Once a month	2.8	
Once a year	2.4	
Never	2.8	
	99.9	
Religiosity Scale:		(*n* = 207)
Intensely religious	45.4	
Religious	30.9	
Moderately religious	20.3	
Minimally religious	3.4	
	100.0	

traditional society, as some theorists suggest, the transformation of rural Libyan society will be a difficult task indeed.

It is interesting to note, however, that Col. Qadafi is himself a devoutly religious individual who has placed the glorification of Islam on a par with the economic modernization of Libya. While attempting to crush the tribal system and radically transform mass behavior patterns, he has simultaneously elevated Koranic strictures to the status of national law. If Libya's Socialist leaders and the development theorists agree on the premise that economic and political development inevitably requires the transformation of traditional societies, they differ markedly on the role of religion in that transformation.

Particularism

The particularism scale consisted of the two items indicated by the factor analysis to best reflect internal group solidarity and hostility toward individuals beyond the immediate confines of the respondent's family or religious groups. Percentage distributions for the particularism scale are presented in Table 4-2. Scale scores ranged from 2 through 8, with 2 representing the most particularistic response and 8 the least. Respondents receiving scores 1, 2 or 3 were considered intensely particularistic; 4 moderately particularistic; 5 minimally particularistic; and 6 through 8 nonparticularistic.

The results of a third item relating to particularism but suggested by the factor analysis as reflecting other dimensions of traditional behavior in addition to particularism has also been included in Table 4-2. It has not, however, been included in the particularism scale.

In general, the intense category on the particularism scale consisted of those individuals who interacted with individuals outside the family less than once a week, and who, in a more general sense, were wary of individuals who rejected prevailing religious norms. The least particularistic individuals were those individuals who interact several times a week with individuals outside of the family, and who were willing to tolerate deviance from prevailing norms. With 81 percent of the respondents falling into the intensely particularistic or particularistic categories, one can only conclude that rural Libya clearly remains a family centered, particularistic society.

Atomism

As noted above, only one of the questionnaire items loaded on the factor we have chosen to label atomism, thereby precluding the development of an atomism scale. Our lone indicator of atomism requested respondents to agree or disagree with a highly atomistic proverb, the text and percentage distributions for which

Table 4-2
Particularism Among Rural Libyans

	Percentage	
About how frequently do you get together in the evening with people outside your family?		(n = 211)
About once a month	39.3	
About once a week, or a few times a month	39.3	
Several times a week	15.6	
Almost every evening	5.7	
	99.9	
How true is the statement religious people are the most trustful, respected, and friendly people in the community?		(n = 210)
True for all religious people	31.0	
True for most	47.1	
True for some	21.4	
True for none	.5	
	100.0	
People outside the family can't be trusted at all. (not included in particularism scale)		(n = 210)
Strongly agree	15.7	
Agree	41.9	
Disagree	30.0	
Strongly Disagree	12.4	
	100.0	
Particularism Scale:		(n = 210)
Intensely particularistic	42.4	
Particularistic	35.6	
Minimally particularistic	11.0	
Non-particularistic	11.0	
	100.0	

appear in Table 4-3. On this basis of their responses to this single item, rural Libyans do not appear to be excessively atomistic.

We would suggest, however, that our single measure of atomism was particularly stringent, and that the fact that 32 percent of the respondents were willing to agree with a proverb suggesting that only their horses require grass was, in itself, an interesting finding. At the very least, the subject of atomistic attitudes is clearly worth further study.

Table 4-3
Atomistic Attitudes among Rural Libyans

	Percentage	
What do you think of the saying that all the people say, "Oh God there is nobody but myself and that after my horse, there is no need for grass"?		($n = 210$)
Strongly agree	9.5	
Agree	23.3	
Disagree	35.7	
Strongly disagree	31.4	
	99.9	

Fatalism

The fatalism scale was similarly based upon the respondents' acceptance or rejection of standard proverbs. In this instance, respondents were asked to choose between contrasting sets of fatalistic and nonfatalistic proverbs, the text and percentage distributions for which appear in Table 4-4. Scores on the

Table 4-4
Fatalism among Rural Libyans

	Percentage	
Place a check mark beside one of the following two proverbs with which you agree.		($n = 209$)
(a) Nothing happens without the will of God.	79.4	
(b) (God says) If man tries, I will help Him.	20.6	
	100.0	
Place a check mark beside one of the following proverbs with which you agree.		($n = 208$)
(a) Livelihoods are divided by God.	86.6	
(b) The poor man is responsible for his own poverty.	12.9	
	99.5	
Fatalism Scale:		($n = 208$)
Intense fatalism	69.2	
Moderate fatalism	28.4	
Low fatalism	2.4	
	100.0	

fatalism scale ranged from 2 (complete agreement on both fatalistic proverbs) through 4 (complete agreement with both nonfatalistic proverbs). Our rural respondents manifested clear fatalistic tendencies, with approximately 70 percent of the sample indicating complete agreement with both fatalistic proverbs.

Interpersonal Distrust

The interpersonal distrust scale was based upon responses to three items, the text and percentage distribution for which appear in Table 4-5.

Scores on the interpersonal distrust scale ranged from 3, indicating complete agreement with all distrust oriented statements, through 6, indicating complete disagreement with both trust oriented statements. As hypothesized

Table 4-5
Interpersonal Distrust Among Rural Libyans

	Percentage	
Check one of the following which suits your judgment:		(n = 211)
(a) Most people can't be trusted.	52.7	
(b) You can't be too careful in your dealings with others.	47.3	
	100.0	
Would you say that most people are more inclined to help others, or more inclined to look out for themselves?		(n = 211)
(a) Help others.	33.7	
(b) Look out for themselves.	65.9	
	100.0	
What do you think of the saying that, "If you were not a wolf, other wolves would eat you".		(n = 208)
Agree	87.5	
Disagree	12.5	
	100.0	
Interpersonal Distrust Scale:		(n = 180)
High Trust	4.4	
Moderate Trust	20.6	
Moderate Distrust	43.9	
Intense Distrust	31.1	
	100.0	

by the earlier discussion, manifestations of interpersonal distrust were clearly evident among the rural sample.

Tribalism

The questionnaire also contained several items relating to tribalism, the text and percentage distributions for which appear in Table 4-6.

All tribal items reflect intense tribalism among rural Libyans. The fact that the tribal system had been abolished by the government prior to the survey, however, resulted in a nonresponse rate of almost 40 percent for the tribalism items, making the results difficult to interpret. Because of the high nonresponse rate, the tribal items were not scaled.

Without exception, then, rural Libyans did appear to conform to the

Table 4-6
Tribalism among Rural Libyans

	Percentage	
If yes (Do you belong to a tribe?) to what extent do you feel loyal and attached to your tribe?		(n = 118)
Very attached	38.1	
Attached	39.8	
Somewhat attached	5.9	
Not attached	16.1	
	99.9	
Do you feel proud to belong to your tribe?		(n = 118)
Very proud	44.9	
Proud	27.1	
Somewhat proud	9.3	
Not proud	18.6	
	99.9	
If you had the chance would you like to drop all tribal identification?		(n = 115)
Yes	31.3	
No	68.7	
	100.0	
If you had the chance would you like to change to another tribe?		(n = 118)
Yes	25.4	
No	74.6	
	100.0	

attitudinal dimensions of traditional societies described earlier. They were intensely religious, distrustful, fatalistic, particularistic and tribalistic—attitudinal predispositions that clearly support the perpetuation of a traditional social order.

Political Development among Rural Libyans

Based upon their clear manifestations of traditional behavior, one would expect Libya's rural citizens to manifest substantial opposition to the political initiatives of the revolutionary government. In order to test this proposition, the ensuing section will examine the responses of rural Libyans to four dimensions of political development: (1) preference for political leaders selected on the basis of achievement rather than on the basis of ascription, (2) attitudinal predisposition to support administrative personnel, (3) an awareness and positive evaluation of regime efforts to improve the standard of life of all Libyan citizens, and (4) participation in the political system.

Political Development Expressed as Preference for Achievement Oriented Leaders

Fundamental to all development theories is the premise that positions of leadership must be filled on the basis of achievement or merit.[6] As long as such ascriptive criteria as lineage dominate the process of elite recruitment, a society will necessarily underutilize its human resources by precluding the advancement of its most talented individuals to positions of leadership. Moreover, both development theorists and Libya's revolutionary leaders have assumed that ascriptive tribal and lineage elites would resist reform programs designed to transform the rural, family centered, largely illiterate society upon which tribal authority is structured into an urban, industrialized, bureaucratically centralized entity in which the roles traditionally played by tribal leaders were totally absorbed by the state. (This assumption is examined at length in the following chapter.)

In so doing, both development theorists and the revolutionary government have also assumed that the strongest support for the traditional ascriptive lineage and religious elites does lie among the rural, illiterate segments of the population.

In order to test this proposition, respondents were asked to identify the one or two individuals they felt were best suited to run their village and then to indicate the major reasons for their selections.

Of the 211 rural, uneducated Libyans sampled, 77.4 percent overwhelmingly selected individuals clearly identifiable as members of the traditional tribal elite structure as individuals best suited to run their village.[7]

Both the development theorists and Libya's revolutionary leaders were accurate, then, in assuming a strong preference for traditional leaders among Libya's predominantly rural and illiterate populations. Perhaps even more illuminating in this regard are the attributes listed as the basis for leadership preference. As indicated in Table 4-7, 59.2 percent of the traditional sample listed purely ascriptive attributes in judging their leadership preference. An additional 27.2 percent listed a combination of ascriptive and achievement attributes, with only 13.6 percent of the rural respondents listing wholly achievement based criteria for leadership selection.

To further pursue this stage of the analysis, responses to the items were merged into a leadership preference scale with individuals citing a purely traditional individual as their leadership choice and citing purely ascriptive attributes as the basis of their choice falling in the most traditional category and individuals listing nontraditional administrations as their leadership preference and justifying this choice on the basis of purely achievement attributes falling in the most modern category.

The marginal distributions for the leadership preference scale indicate that 54 percent of the rural respondents manifested strong ascriptive leadership preferences, while a mere 8 percent indicated a preference for leaders with purely achievement values. These figures offer strong support for the proposition that members of Libya's rural, uneducated population do, indeed, provide a strong basis of popular support for the traditional elite structure.

Table 4-7
Leadership Preference among Rural Libyans

	Percentage	
Preferred Elites		(*n* = 195)
Ascriptive	77.4	
Achievement	22.6	
	100.0	
Preferred Leadership Attributes		(*n* = 191)
Ascriptive	59.2	
Mixed	27.2	
Achievement	13.6	
	100.0	
Leadership Preference Scale:		(*n* = 190)
Ascriptive	53.7	
Mixed	37.9	
Modern	8.4	
	100.0	

*Political Development as Affective Support
for Government Officials*

In Libya, as in most developing areas, the burden of economic and social development falls squarely upon the government. It is the government that must stimulate industrial development, build schools, establish health and welfare programs, initiate agricultural extension programs, and generally generate and supervise the massive transformation of Libyan society envisioned by the revolutionary leadership. The effectiveness of the government in guiding this transformation and mobilizing the local population in support of its developmental objectives depends in large measure upon the level of trust of effective support for public officials among the population. If the local administrators are trusted and well regarded, they can serve as invaluable links in the process of overcoming inertia to change by persuading rural populations of the benefits of change and by inducing them to give reform programs a chance to demonstrate their value. If, to the contrary, local public officials are the object of doubt and hostility, their utility in promoting social and economic reform is likely to be nil.

In the context of this chapter, both development theorists and the revolutionary government have assumed that rural population would oppose modernizing administrators who attempted to disrupt established social patterns by promoting economic and social reform. Indeed, as will be noted in Chapter 6, the revolutionary government's pessimism in this regard led to a scrapping of concerted attempts to build a modernizing core of local administrators less than two years after its initiation.

To test the proposition that Libya's rural and uneducated population were, indeed, hostile to the modernizing public administrators, the rural respondents were asked a battery of questions relating to their evaluation of both the mayors of their respective villages and local officials in general. It should be noted that all of the mayors in question were "modernizers" appointed by the revolutionary government to stimulate the economic and social development of the area. This was also partially true of the public officials. In most instances they had replaced ascriptive tribal administrations and generally had few ties with the tribal rural elite.

Tables 4-8 and 4-9 survey evaluations by the rural respondents of their mayors and local administrators, respectively. Combined scales were also constructed for each set of items and appear at the bottom of each table. Break points for the scales are footnoted.

The percentages presented in Tables 4-8 and 4-9 indicate uneducated Libyans manifested minimal hostility to the mayors and administration appointed by the central government. Perhaps a reluctance on the part of many respondents

Table 4-8
Evaluations of Mayors by Rural Libyans

	Percentage	
The mayor runs the town to suit himself.		(n = 202)
Very true	19.8	
True	36.6	
Untrue	33.2	
Very untrue	10.4	
	100.0	
The mayor gets very little done.		(n = 206)
Very true	18.4	
True	35.0	
Untrue	35.9	
Very untrue	10.7	
	100.0	
The mayor does not represent the community at all.		(n = 200)
Very true	15.0	
True	31.5	
Untrue	43.0	
Very untrue	10.5	
	100.0	
The mayor is not accepted by the majority of the community.		(n = 202)
Very true	15.8	
True	37.6	
Untrue	38.6	
Very untrue	7.9	
	99.9	
Mayor Performance Scale:[a]		(n = 196)
Bad	15.8	
Poor	32.7	
Good	37.8	
Excellent	13.8	
	99.4	

[a]Possible scores of the Mayor Performance Scale ranged from 4 through 16, with score of 4 indicating total approval of the mayor's performance, score of 16 indicating total rejection. Scores ranging from 4 through 6 were considered excellent evaluations of the mayor's performance; 7 through 9, good; 10 through 12, poor; 13 through 16, bad.

Table 4-9
Evaluations of Local and Provincial Administrations by Rural Libyans

	Percentage	
They are popular and trusted by the public.		(n = 201)
Yes	63.7	
No	36.3	
	100.0	
They have the ability and quality of leadership.		(n = 202)
Yes	65.8	
No	34.2	
	100.0	
They are dedicated and decisive in their work.		(n = 203)
Yes	63.5	
No	36.5	
	100.0	
They represent the majority of the community.		(n = 201)
Yes	57.2	
No	42.8	
	100.0	
Administration Performance Scale:[a]		(n = 194)
Bad	23.7	
Poor	8.8	
Good	22.2	
Excellent	45.4	
	100.1	

[a]Possible scores on the Administrator Performance Scale ranged from 4 through 8, with scores of 4 indicating a positive evaluation on all items, a score of 8 indicating a negative evaluation. Scores of 4 were considered excellent evaluations of the administrator's performance; 5 and 6, good; 7, poor; 8, bad.

to criticize the government may have disguised some latent hostility toward the local administrative structure.

Nevertheless, the percentages in Tables 4-8 and 4-9 fail to reflect the pervasive opposition to local administrators that both the development theorists and the revolutionary government anticipated. What the figures do reflect, however, is that the local administration did lack sufficiently broad popular support to generate any real enthusiasm for the new and innovative programs. To be tolerated by the mass is not necessarily to lead. If the social and economic transformation programs are to be successful, greater popular receptiveness to the public officials involved is clearly essential.

Political Development as Support of Regime Goals

Yet a third measure of the political development of a society is the extent to which the polity shares the basic values of the dominant elite. In this regard, it is almost axiomatic to suggest that the more individuals share regime values the more readily they can be mobilized in support of its programs. Again, both development theorists and Libya's revolutionary leaders have assumed the rural population to be opposed to the goals of political and economic modernization.

To test the proposition that uneducated rural Libyans were opposed to the economic and social reforms sponsored by the revolutionary leadership, respondents were requested to evaluate the effectiveness of various government reform programs. In this regard it was felt that evaluative assessments of the various reform programs would reflect both the individual's attitude toward modernization programs in general and the impact of the government's social and economic reforms in building legitimizing support for the regime and its policies. This is particularly the case inasmuch as the revolutionary government has made provision of "cradle-to-grave" welfare services to all areas of the country one of its top priorities.

Table 4-10 reflects levels of support for government reform and welfare measures in four areas: agriculture, health, housing, and education. Break points for the respective scales are provided in the footnotes.

Contrary to our expectations, the percentages appearing in Table 4-10 reflect considerable recognition among rural uneducated Libyans of the efforts of the revolutionary government to improve their lot.

To pursue the theme, respondents were also requested to indicate the extent of their participation in government assistance and reform programs. It was felt that this was a particularly important item, for without extensive mass involvement, the impact of reform programs in effecting radical social and economic transformations is likely to be minimal. Levels of rural involvement in government assistance programs is reflected in the items appearing in Table 4-11.

Quite clearly, rural Libyans have not been penetrated by government reform programs. It is difficult to ascertain whether this marked lack of rural involvement is due to public resistance or to a lack of an adequate administrative capacity to reach the rural areas. Whatever the cause, Libya's rural populations must be penetrated if the social and economic transformations envisioned by the revolutionary government are to be achieved.

Table 4-10
Levels of Support for Government Reform and Welfare Measures

	Percentage	
Agriculture		
Farmers get all the assistance they need to increase and improve their production.		(*n* 204)
Strongly agree	19.6	
Agree	64.2	
Disagree	14.7	
Strongly disagree	1.5	
	100.0	
The farmer's standard of living is going up as never before.		(*n* = 206)
Strongly agree	28.6	
Agree	58.3	
Disagree	12.1	
Strongly disagree	1.0	
	100.0	
Most of the agricultural problems are taken care of by our government.		(*n* = 207)
Strongly agree	23.2	
Agree	56.0	
Disagree	19.3	
Strongly disagree	1.4	
	99.9	
Agricultural Satisfaction Scale:[a]		(*n* = 203)
Excellent	10.8	
Very good	20.2	
Good	55.2	
Poor/bad	13.8	
	100.0	
Health		
Local government provides approaches to improving the health of the entire community.		(*n* = 208)
Strongly agree	14.4	
Agree	36.5	
Disagree	18.3	
Strongly disagree	30.8	
	100.0	
Medical care and hospitalization is readily available to the community.		(*n* = 209)
Strongly agree	12.0	
Agree	43.1	

Table 4-10 — Continued

	Percentage	
Disagree	39.7	
Strongly disagree	5.3	
	100.1	

Health Satisfaction Scale:[b]   (n = 208)

Excellent	14.4
Good	36.5
Poor	18.3
Bad	30.8
	100.0

Housing and Transportation

We have good housing and plans for improvement of residential areas.   (n = 208)

Strongly agree	8.7
Agree	44.2
Disagree	33.2
Strongly disagree	13.9
	100.0

We have good recreational areas.   (n = 208)

Strongly agree	8.2
Agree	42.8
Disagree	31.7
Strongly disagree	17.3
	100.0

We have good highways, traffic, transportation, and other facilities are under way in our community.   (n = 208)

Strongly agree	8.2
Agree	42.3
Disagree	31.7
Strongly disagree	17.8
	100.0

Housing/Transportation Satisfaction Scale:[c]   (n = 208)

Excellent	8.2
Good	44.2
Poor	28.4
Bad	19.2
	100.0

Education

Our teachers are highly qualified and dedicated.   (n = 201)

Strongly agree	19.4

Table 4-10 — Continued

	Percentage
Agree	61.2
Disagree	16.4
Strongly disagree	3.0
	100.0
Our schools have good facilities for modern education and are generally in good condition. ($n = 203$)	
Strongly agree	17.7
Agree	53.7
Disagree	24.6
Strongly disagree	3.9
	99.9
Education Satisfaction Scale:[d] ($n = 198$)	
Excellent	20.7
Good	43.9
Poor	21.7
Bad	13.6
	99.9

[a]Possible scores on the Agricultural Satisfaction Scale ranged from 3 through 12, with 3 indicating high satisfaction on items and 12 indicating nonsatisfaction on all items. Scores of 3 were considered excellent; 4 and 5, good; 6 and 7, poor; 8 through 12, bad.

[b]Possible scores on the Health Satisfaction Scale ranged from 2 through 8, with 2 indicating the highest possible satisfaction, 8 the least. Scores of 2 or 3 were considered excellent, 4, good; 5, poor; 6 through 8, bad.

[c]Possible scores on the Housing/Transportation Satisfaction Scale ranged from 3 through 12, with 3 indicating the highest level of satisfaction, 12 the lowest. Scores ranging from 3 to 5 were considered excellent; 6 and 7, good; 8 and 9, poor; 10 through 12, bad.

[d]Possible scores on the Education Satisfaction Scale ranged from 2 through 8, with 2 indicating maximum satisfaction and 8 indicating minimal satisfaction. Scores of 2 and 3 were considered excellent; 4, good; 5, poor; and 6 through 8, bad.

Political Development as Political Participation

One of the prime indicators of political development is political participation. People who participate are aware of the political system. They are involved and available for mobilization by the dominant elite. Rural uneducated populations are assumed to be the least participatory segment of society and, accordingly, the most difficult to link to national political institutions. To test the propositions that Libya's rural uneducated population is largely nonparticipatory and to examine the success of the revolutionary government in establishing

Table 4-11
Rural Participation in Government Modernization Programs

	Percentage	
How often have you received any assistance from the government?		(n = 211)
Many times	7.1	
Once or twice	23.7	
Never	69.2	
	100.0	
What type(s) of assistance have you received?		(n = 211)
Agriculture		
Yes	23.2	
No	76.8	
	100.0	(n = 211)
Education		
Yes	000.0	
No	100.0	
	100.0	(n = 211)
Housing		
Yes	3.8	
No	96.2	
	100.0	(n = 211)
Welfare		
Yes	4.7	
No	95.3	
	100.0	

participatory links with Libya's predominantly rural mass, the questionnaire contained items relating both to the individual's attitudinal predisposition to become politically involved and the individual's actual level of political involvement with diverse agencies of the Libyan government. Both the attitudinal and overt participation items were scaled to produce more general participation indicators. The text and percentage distributions for both the individual participation items and the composite scales appear in Table 4-12. Break points for the scales are footnoted.

The percentages presented in Table 4-12 clearly indicate that rural Libyans do not participate in the political system. At least as of 1974, the revolutionary government had largely failed to bridge the gap between the local political leadership and the rural mass. Realization of this fact undoubtedly figured strongly in the government's decision to launch the "popular revolution" and "People's Congresses" described in some detail in Chapter 6.

Table 4-12
Political Participation Among Rural Libyans

	Percentage	
Only those who are competent on issues should speak.		(n = 143)
Strongly agree	18.9	
Agree	57.3	
Disagree	21.7	
Strongly disagree	2.1	
	100.0	
Widespread participation in decision making often leads to undesirable conflicts.		(n = 145)
Strongly agree	13.1	
Agree	46.2	
Disagree	35.2	
Strongly disagree	5.5	
	100.0	
Participation of the people is not necessary if decision making is left in the hands of a few trusted and competent leaders.		(n = 145)
Strongly agree	16.6	
Agree	57.9	
Disagree	19.3	
Strongly disagree	6.2	
	100.0	
Political Predisposition Scale:[a]		(n = 143)
Intense	5.6	
Medium high	19.6	
Medium low	55.9	
Very low	18.9	
	100.0	
About how many of your relatives or good friends are active in (check one for each)?		
Arab Socialist Union		(n = 211)
Most	3.8	
Some	8.1	
Few	20.4	
None	67.8	
	100.0	
Local Government		(n = 211)
Most	.5	
Some	6.6	
Few	16.1	
None	76.8	
	100.0	

Table 4-12 — Continued

	Percentage	
Central Government		(n = 211)
Most	0	
Some	2.4	
Few	5.7	
None	91.9	
	100.0	
Community Organizations		(n = 211)
Most	.9	
Some	4.3	
Few	10.4	
None	84.4	
	100.0	
Overt Participation Scale:[b]		(n = 211)
Very high	1.4	
High	4.3	
Moderate	10.0	
Low	25.6	
None	58.8	
	100.0	

[a]Possible scores on the Political Predisposition Scale ranged from 3 through 12, with scores of 3 indicating minimal predisposition to become politically involved and scores of 12 indicating maximum predisposition. Scores ranging from 8 to 5 were considered very low; 6 and 7, low; 8 and 9, high; and 10 through 12, very high.

[b]Possible scores on the Overt Participation Scale ranged from 4 through 16, with scores of 4 indicating maximum contact with the political system and scores of 16 minimal contact. Scores of 4 were considered intense; 5 through 9, high; 10 and 11, moderate; 12 and 13, low; 14 through 16, very low.

A Comparison of the Political Attitudes of Rural and Less Rural Populations

The final stage of our analysis involved analyzing the extent to which the political behavior of rural Libyans differed from that of individuals possessing a broader exposure to urbanization, education, and the mass media. Though far from being a perfect indicator, the attitude and behavior patterns of transitional and modern Libyans may provide the best indicator available of the attitudes and behavior likely to characterize Libya's rural populations once they encounter the full impact of the government's modernization programs. If the attitudes characteristic of transitional and modern segments of the Libyan population are clearly supportive of the regime and its modernization programs, this information should serve as a source of positive reinforcement to the revolutionary leadership and provide some indication that its modernization programs are on target.

If, however, the attitudes and behavior patterns that characterize Libya's transitional and modern citizens are not particularly supportive of the regime and its modernization efforts, Libya's modernizing leaders may wish either to reduce the pace of their social transformation policies and shift their emphasis to gaining greater control over the attitudes instilled by the change process or revamp the content of the education system, the mass media, and other agents of political socialization.

Toward this end, the attitudes and behavior patterns of our sample of uneducated rural Libyans were correlated with the behavior patterns manifested by their transitional and modern counterparts. Gamma coefficients resulting from these correlations are presented in Table 4-13. Positive correlations indicate that the more modern respondents manifested attitudes and behavior patterns more supportive of Libya's revolutionary leaders and their programs than those manifested by our sample of rural Libyans. Negative correlations indicate that the traditional rural sample was more supportive of the revolutionary regime and its programs than their more modern brethren.

The coefficients presented in Table 4-13 suggested the following observations. In reference to the traditional attitudes and behavior patterns discussed in the initial section of the analysis, it is clear that "modern Libyans" are far less atomistic, fatalistic, and particularistic than their traditional brethren. "Modern" Libyans, however, were not significantly less religious than traditional rural Libyans, nor did they score much higher in terms of interpersonal trust.

In reference to the indicators of political development, the main focus of the chapter, some very interesting trends occur. The more modern Libyans are clearly more supportive of leaders selected on the basis of achievement and merit than the rural Libyans who, as noted earlier, continue to manifest a strong preference for ascriptive leaders. Modern Libyans were also far more likely to participate in the government and its political agencies, such as the Arab Socialist Union, than their rural counterparts. To this degree the government's education and media programs appear to be building regime support.

On the negative side, the better educated Libyans and those with the greatest exposure to the press and television are less likely than their rural counterparts to display positive evaluations toward local or regional administrators. They are also less likely to manifest satisfaction with government reform programs designed to build support for the regime and to demonstrate its utility. If anything, education and the mass media have increased demands rather than supports. While this trend is not strong, it does indicate that educating individuals and exposing them to greater information does not necessarily build support for the regime.

Table 4-13
Information Exposure and Support for Political Modernization*

	n	Religio-sity	Particu-larism	Fatalism	Inter-Personal Distrust	Atomism	Leadership Preference	Mayor	Adminis-trator	Agricul-ture	Edu-cation	Resident	Health	Accepted Government Assistance	Attitu-dinal Partici-pation	Overt Partici-pation
Demographic Scale[a] (Education, Urbanization, Television, Exposure)	576	G =[b] 0.175	0.460	0.400	0.257	0.643	G =[c] 0.453	0.228	−0.151	0.091	−0.365	−0.111	0.218	0.245	0.245	0.466
Urbanization		0.097	0.293	0.247	0.398	0.646	0.333	0.178	−0.075	0.157	−0.187	−0.129	0.168		0.245	0.444
Education		0.211	0.501	0.473	0.156	0.629	0.451	0.164	−0.202	0.068	−0.329	−0.129	0.142	0.286	0.236	0.460
Television		0.265	0.468	0.338	0.244	0.578	0.387	0.180	−0.189	0.032	−0.414	−0.117	0.123	0.253	0.148	0.403
Newspaper		0.284	0.556	0.488	0.157	0.684	0.515	0.171	−0.202	0.059	−0.427	−0.124	0.145	0.403	0.283	0.578
Ability to Recall Recent Political Events		0.060	0.313	0.296	0.074	0.246	0.468	0.026	−0.091	0.018	−0.069	−0.113	0.156	0.032	0.440	0.469
Ability to Identify Local and Regional Officials		0.174	0.388	0.425	0.202	0.576	0.456	0.009	−0.263	−0.004	−0.221	−0.204	0.022	0.222	0.235	0.466
Age		0.429	0.384	0.249	0.081	0.329	0.224	0.035	−0.162	0.082	−0.217	−0.101	0.055	0.133	0.201	0.153

*Questionnaire items relating to television exposure, urbanization, and media exposure were combined into a Demographic Scale. All three items received equal weight. Possible scale scores ranged from 3 through 9, with 3 indicating rural status with no education or television exposure and 9 representing the highest categories of urbanization, education, and television exposure. Scores of 3 or 4 were considered traditional; scores of 5, 6, or 7, transitional; scores of 8 or 9, modern.

[a]Gamma Coefficients. All Coefficients over ± .200 are significant at the .05 level or beyond. Coefficients were based upon a pairwise deletion of cases.

[b]Positive Coefficients indicate a positive correlation between the independent variables relating to greater exposure to "modern" information and either a decrease in traditional attitudes or positive support for government modernization programs. Negative coefficients indicate that greater exposure to modern information either strengthened traditional attitudes or resulted in a negative reaction to governmental modernization programs.

Notes

1. Daniel Lerner, *The Passing of Traditional Society* (Glencoe, Ill.: Free Press, 1958), chaps. 2, 3.
2. Questionnaire items relating to television exposure, urbanization, and media exposure were combined into a Demographic Scale. All three items received equal weight. Possible scale scores ranged from 3 through 9, with 3 indicating rural status with no education or television exposure and 9 representing the highest categories of urbanization, education, and television exposure. Scores of 3 or 4 were considered traditional; scores of 5, 6, or 7, transitional; scores of 8 or 9, modern.
3. Gabriel A. Almond and Sidney Verba, *Civic Culture* (Boston: Little, Brown, 1963).

Talcott Parsons, *Structure of Social Action* (Glencoe, Ill.: Free Press, 1949).

Gideon Sjorberg, "The Rural-Urban Dimension in Preindustrial, Transitional, and Industrial Societies," in Robert E. L. Faris, ed., *Handbook of Modern Sociology* (Chicago: Rand McNally, 1964), pp. 127-159.

Ferdinand Tonnies, *Community and Society Gemeinschaft and Gesellschaft.* Translated and edited by C. P. Loomis (East Lansing: Michigan State University Press, 1947).

F. X. Sutton, "Social Theory and Comparative Politics", in Harry Eckstein and David E. Apter, eds., *Comparative Politics* (Glencoe, Ill.: Free Press, 1963), pp. 67-82.

Gideon Sjoberg, "Folk and Feudal Societies," *American Journal of Sociology,* 58 (November 1952): 231-239; Hehmet Beqiraj, Peasantry in Revolution (Ithaca, N.Y.: Cornell University Press, 1966).

Everett E. Hagen, *On the Theory of Social Change* (Homewood, Ill.: Dorsey Press, 1962), pp. 68-69, 124-157.

John C. McKinney, *Constructive Typology and Social Theory* (New York: Appleton-Century-Crofts, 1966).

Helio Jaguaribe, *Political Development: A General Theory and a Latin American Case Study* (New York: Harper & Row, 1973).

W. W. Rostow, *The Process of Economic Growth,* 2nd ed. (New York: W. W. Norton, 1952, 1962) p. 307. With permission of publisher.

Joseph A. Kahl, *The Measurement of Modernism: A Study of Values in Brazil and Mexico,* Latin American Monographs, No. 12 (Austin, Tex.: Institute of Latin American Studies, University of Texas, 1968); David Horton Smith and Alex Inkeles, "The OM Scale: A Comparative Socio-Psychological Measure of Individual Modernity," *Sociometry* 29 (December 1966): 353-77.

Numerous examples of this situation can be found in Kalman H. Silvert, ed., *Expectant Peoples* (New York: Random House, 1963); Kuswin Nair, *Blossoms in the Dust* (London: C. Duckworth, 1961); George Dalton, ed., *Economic*

Development and Social Change: The Modernization of Village Communities (Garden City, N.Y.: The Natural History Press, 1971).

Samuel P. Huntington, *Political Order in Changing Societies* (New Haven: Yale University Press, 1968).

S. N. Eisenstadt, "Convergence and Divergence of Modern and Modernizing Societies: Indications from the Analysis of the Structuring of Social Hierarchies in Middle Eastern Societies", *International Journal of Middle East Studies* 8 (1977): 1-27.

David E. Apter, *The Politics of Modernization* (Chicago: University of Chicago Press, 1965), pp. 100-122.

4. Ibid.

5. PA2, Oblique; $n = 576$. Pairwise delection of cases.

6. See note 3.

7. For operationalization of traditional rural elites, see Chapter 5.

5

Opposition to Social Change Among Traditional Libyan Elites
Omar I. El Fathaly and *Monte Palmer*

In the fall of 1969 the Libyan monarchy was overthrown by a group of young military officers headed by Muammar Qadafi. In the months prior to the revolution the tribal-based monarchy had found it difficult to cope with the stress of rapid social and economic change, and had found itself immobilized by the conflict between Libya's traditional tribal and religious elite and a small but influential modernizing elite composed of students, technocrats, and younger military officers. This new elite, a by-product of Libya's oil wealth, had become particularly distressed by the arbitrariness and inefficiency of the monarchy, the severe maldistribution of the oil revenues, and the existence of what they felt to be a poorly planned and managed development program which had largely failed to penetrate Libya's predominantly rural areas.

In their statements, the newly formed Revolutionary Command Council (RCC) vowed to create a new society built upon "the principles of freedom, justice, unity, modernization and socialism."[1] The creation of this new society, the RCC said, required the dismantling of existing administrative structures at all levels, and their replacement with new institutions and personnel better suited to the needs of a modernizing society.

Local administrative units at the time of the revolution, they explained, were the de facto boundaries of Libya's major tribes.[2] Local administrative officials were tribal sheikhs or their appointees. Their positions were inherited as an ascriptive right. They owed little to the central government. Their legitimacy in the eyes of the masses was based upon family status, wealth, and symbols of religious piety. Moreover, the ignorance of the masses and their pervasive sense of fatalism made it unlikely that the ascriptive basis of the tradition rural elites would ever be effectively challenged from below.

Traditional rural elites, the RCC continued, could not be counted on to lead Libya's transformation into a modern Socialist state. They were jealous of their authority and very aware of its tribal and religious foundations. They would view modernization programs as a threat, and would use their authority with the masses to impair their progress. Moreover, traditional rural elites did not think in modern terms. In background, experience, and values they were part of the past.

This chapter originally appeared in Volume 8 of the *International Journal of Middle Eastern Studies*. Reprinted with permission.

In assuming Libya's traditional rural elites to be hostile to rapid social and economic modernization, the RCC has followed a path well charted by Socialist-oriented leaders throughout the developing areas. Within the Middle Eastern context, for example, this clearly has been the assumption of modernizing leaders in Egypt, Syria, Iraq, Tunisia, and Algeria. It is also an assumption that has found justification in most theories of social, economic, and political development. Beginning with Tonnies's *Gemeinschaft and Gesellschaft* and continuing through Weber's dichotomization of traditional and rational-legal authority, Parsons "pattern variables," and Almond and Verba's parochial and particularistic cultures, virtually all theoretical works on development have stressed the antithetical nature of the traditional and the modern worlds.[3]

Traditionalism and modernity, as employed by both Colonel Qadafi and most social theorists, represent alternative modes of social organization.[4] Defined in terms of their major characteristics, traditional societies are predominantly rural, family-based, tribal societies engaged in agrarian pursuits such as herding or subsistence agriculture. The mass of the population are illiterate and have been socialized onto traditions that venerate the past, resist change, and focus primary loyalties upon the family and tribal units. Social and political status are ascribed on the basis of lineage. Mobility across status lines is virtually nil. Education, occupational mobility, technological innovation, mass political participation, and other avenues of social and political change are discouraged by both cultural mores and the self-interest of the dominant elements of society.

Modern societies, by contrast, are urban and industrial. The state is the focal point of citizen loyalty. Education is pervasive; innovation is prized. Status and occupational mobility are fluid. Authority is allocated on the basis of achievement rather than ascribed virtues. Mass political participation is stressed.

For purposes of this chapter, *traditional* and *modern* refer to the ideal-type societies outlined above and extensively developed in works such as Hagen's *Toward a Theory of Social Change*, McKinney's *Constructive Typology and Social Theory*, and Jaquaribe's *Political Development*.[5] *Modernization* refers to the transition of societies from a predominantly traditional form of social organization to a predominantly modern form of social organization.[6] *Traditional elites*, in line with the definitions, are elites that have attained their positions of authority primarily on the basis of their lineage and other forms of ascribed status. *Modernizing leaders* are those political leaders who have, whatever their origins, manifested a commitment to the accelerated transition of their societies from the traditional to the modern form of social organization. Operational definitions of traditional and modernizing elites are provided in the body of the chapter.

Even works which question the antithetical delineation of tradition and modernity, it should be stressed, do not deny that fundamental differences exist between traditional and modern societies. Rather, they suggest that there are many facets of traditional life that could, with effort, be adapted to the pursuit of modernization.⁷ Most importantly, they suggest that if traditional elites could be co-opted into the modernization process, it would place the weight of tradition on the side of modernization and would avoid the problem of forcing rural populations to choose between the demands of their traditional leaders and those of the modernization process.

In spite of the RCC's deep suspicion of the traditional elites, the inability of the modernizing administrations to generate popular acceptance for RCC reform programs as well as RCC's uncertainty over the results of the popular revolution also caused members of the RCC to at least ponder the utility of co-opting the traditional rural elites into the reform process. Accordingly, in the fall of 1973, a research project was initiated to (1) evaluate the attitudes toward social change of those traditional rural elites that possessed the greatest standing among the rural populations and (2) ascertain the nature of their popular support. This chapter is based upon the results of that project.

The objectives of this chapter are (1) to provide an empirical profile of Libya's traditional rural elites and the extent to which they fit the model of traditional rural elites delineated by the RCC and the development theorists surveyed; (2) to ascertain the extent to which the background characteristics of the rural elites have resulted in general attitudinal predispositions against change; (3) to examine attitudes of the rural elites toward government-sponsored modernization programs; (4) to study the quantity of the popular support of the rural elites and the extent to which it is based upon their ascriptive attributes, and (5) based upon the analysis, to bring empirical data to bear on the broader question of adaptability of traditional elites to the modernization process.

Methodology

In the fall of 1973, as noted in the introduction, a questionnaire of 337 items was orally administered to a random sample of 10 percent ($n = 576$) of the adult males residing in seven villages in the Libyan province of Zavia. Ages of the respondents ranged from nineteen to sixty-six, with 55 percent of those in the sample being under the age of forty-two. Eighty-nine percent of those in the sample were married.

Respondents in the seven villages were asked to identify those one or two individuals best qualified to run their village. It was felt that this technique, one well established in studies of local elites in the United States, would best identify those local leaders, traditional and otherwise, who possessed the strongest basis of popular support and who, accordingly, would be in the best position to influence popular attitudes for or against the RCC's modernization programs.⁸ The respondents were also asked to state the rationale for their selections as well as to answer a variety of questions relating to their socioeconomic backgrounds and to their attitudes toward social and economic change.

In each instance, one or two individuals were identified by 90 or more percent of the respondents as being the natural leader of their village. Of fourteen names to emerge from this process, ten were of individuals who had dominated local politics during the monarchy and who thereby met the operational definition of traditional rural elites suggested by Libya's revolutionary leaders.

The ten individuals falling in the category of traditional elites were then interviewed in depth to ascertain their background characteristics, their general predispositions toward change, their ability to conceptualize village problems in an innovative way, their receptiveness to government economic modernization projects, and their willingness to cooperate with modernizing administrators appointed by the RCC. The names of the respondents have been withheld in accordance with a pledge of anonymity provided at the time of the interviews.

Traditional Elites in Libya: A Profile

The power of traditional elites, in the view of both Colonel Qadafi and most development theorists, is based upon their lineage, their wealth, and their manipulation of religious symbols. Accordingly, the interviews probed each of these areas.

The results sustained their evaluations. Most were members of tribes that had originated in the Arabian Peninsula, a mark of great distinction within the hierarchy of Libyan tribes. All were members of the largest and wealthiest tribes in the province, size and wealth being key ingredients in a tribe's overall status. All were members of the one or two most dominant families within each tribe; families that traditionally provided the tribe with its leaders and that "managed" if not monopolized a preponderance of the tribe's communal wealth. Half were the eldest sons of tribal chiefs. All had inherited their family's ascribed right to rule. When asked to rank various facets of their attachment to their tribe and to the tribal system on a scale of one to four, all invariably selected the most intense response. All scoff at recent laws allowing individuals to drop their tribal affiliations. Their intense pride in tribal lineage was particularly striking in light of the fact that most of the tribes under consideration had long ago divested themselves of their bedouin trappings and had been transformed into agrarian villages.

In terms of economic status, each of the ten respondents managed personal and tribal landholdings, the former being not fully distinguishable from the latter inasmuch as land in Libya tends to be communal in origin. In addition, the ten respondents either ran major businesses, occupied a variety of bureaucratic positions at the local level, or both. Major businesses in the Libyan context refer to the construction and import-export firms that emerged with the discovery of Libya's vast oil reserves and which have prospered as prime recipients of government and oil-related contracts. Under the monarchy, favored positions in both the business and governmental arena were allocated to the dominant families of the larger and wealthier tribes as one means of assuring their support. The political influence of the major tribes and their dominant families was thus further augmented by Libya's oil prospertiy. This strengthened position of the traditional elites undoubtedly added to the RCC's apprehension concerning their willingness to cooperate with its Socialist-oriented reform programs. Explicit attempts to access the overall wealth of the candidates came to naught.

In the realm of religion, when the ten respondents were asked if they considered themselves to be extremely religious, very religious, somewhat religious, not religious, or noncommitted, all professed to be extremely religious. All prayed at the mosque at least once a day. All had made the holy pilgrimage to Mecca. The pilgrimage, it should be noted, is of particular symbolic importance in rural Libya inasmuch as it epitomizes exceptional piety or rectitude. It is a prerequisite to any claim to ascriptive leadership. It might also be noted that the Libyan monarchy had been founded by a Muslim saint and was, in reality, a theocracy.

The average age of the traditional elites was fifty-two, a very advanced age in the Libyan context. The youngest was forty; the oldest, sixty-two. All thus benefited from the ascriptive title of Sheikh (wise with age).

Finally, the educational background of the traditional elites was minimal. All had received some primary education, but only one had attended college. None had received formal training of any kind outside of Libya. All things considered, there appeared to be little in their educational background that would incline them to support the RCC's modernization programs.

The Legitimacy of Traditional Elites: The View from Below

Colonel Qadafi was essentially correct, then, in contending that Libya's traditional elites based their claim for leadership upon such ascribed virtues as lineage, wealth, rectitude (piety), and age.

The fundamental question involved in evaluating the ability of the traditional Libyan elites to either facilitate or obstruct economic development thus centers on the ability of the traditional elites to manipulate the rural population, that is, the extent to which the local populations are tied to or willing to support the traditional leaders because of their age, religious piety, wealth, lineage, and social status.

To answer this question, respondents in the large public sample of rural Libyans were asked two questions: (1) Would you vote for or actively support the individual you listed as being the person best suited to run this village? and (2) Why?

Of the 354 respondents listing traditional elites as the individuals best suited to run their villages, 349 said they would vote for or otherwise support them; 310 of the 354 respondents also felt they would receive the strong support of all villagers.

In responding to the "why" portion of the question, respondents generally gave one or two reasons for supporting the individual they cited as being the natural leader of the village. The reasons offered for supporting the traditional local elites, listed in the order of the frequency with which they were mentioned, were religious piety, tribal and family lineage, traditional wisdom, respect and social conformity, education, age, and practical experience (Table 5-1).

Overwhelmingly, then, the mass support accruing to the traditional local elites was based upon their ascriptive attributes.

The corresponding reasons listed by respondents supporting the modernizing leaders stressed education, administrative skill, and support for the community projects.

Given the contrasting bases of support of the traditional and modernizing leaders, we were particularly anxious to examine the educational and demographic characteristics of those individuals citing ascriptive attributes as the primary basis for supporting a particular leader. According to logic of the Libyan situation, we hypothesized that the supporters of the traditional elites or other respondents citing purely ascriptive reasons for selecting an individual as being best suited to run their village would be (1) older, (2) less educated, (3) less urbanized, (4) more religious, (5) of lower socioeconomic status, and (6) far more tribal oriented than individuals supporting the appointed modernizing leaders. This point was of interest for several reasons. First, if the traditional leaders found their greatest support among the least economically developed segment of the population,

Table 5-1
Preferred Attributes of Traditional Rural Elites

	Percentage Mentioning[a]	n Mentioning
Religious piety	74.6	264
Lineage, family, tribe	37.5	133
Traditional wisdom	33	118
Sincerity, respect, social conformity	31	111
Education	14	50
Age	4	14
Practical experience	0.6	2

[a]Twenty percent of respondents listed attributes falling in more than one category making a total *n* in excess of 100 percent.

they might feel constrained in pursuing economic and social modernization projects for fear of alienating their supporters. By the same token, if traditional elites perceived that their support decreased as modernization increased, it would clearly be in their rational self-interest to resist modernization. Third, if the hypothesis were sustained, it would indicate that the appointed modernizing leaders had failed to penetrate that very traditional portion of Libyan society in greatest need of change if Libya were to make substantial progress in the area of rural development, and that, in spite of the difficulties involved, working through the traditional elites might yet prove to be the most expeditious means of disseminating technology among the rural masses. And, finally, if the hypothesis were sustained, it would support the assumption made by most development theorists that the support of traditional elites is inversely correlated with such attributes of economic modernization as education, urbanization, and nonagrarian employment. It would also suggest that as economic development progressed, the influence of traditional leaders would collapse of its weight without the need for direct pressure by the central government.

To test this proposition, respondents were divided into traditional, transitional, and modern categories based upon both the background of the individuals they cited as being best able to run their village and the type of attributes they listed as being most important to their leadership selection. Traditional individuals, under this classification, were those individuals either listing purely ascriptive attributes for leadership preference (religious piety, lineage) or citing one of the ten traditional rural elites as the individual best qualified to run the village. Modern individuals were those individuals citing a modernizing administrator as the person best qualified to run the village or citing achievement attributes as the basis for their leadership preference (education, practical experience). Individuals citing attributes such as sincerity, traditional wisdom, and social conformity, who cited both traditional and modern attributes as their basis for citing an individual as being best able to run the village or who cited achievement-oriented attributes as the basis of supporting a member of the traditional elite were termed mixed or transitional.

All facets of the hypothesis were sustained, albeit with varying degrees of intensity. The supporters of the traditional elites or respondents who offered ascriptive reasons for their leadership preference were older, less educated, less urbanized, more religious, of a lower social status, and more intense in their tribal loyalties than the supporters of the modernizing administrators appointed by the RCC.

In terms of age, approximately 33 percent of the respondents under the age of forty preferred traditional local elites or offered ascriptive reasons for supporting a modernizing leader, a figure that jumped to 45 percent among respondents between the ages of forty and sixty-six, and 61 percent among respondents over the age of sixty-six. An additional 33 percent of the twenty to forty age group preferred leaders possessing modern attributes, a figure that dropped to 18 percent among respondents falling in the forty to sixty age group and to 11 percent in the oldest category. Approximately 33 percent in each age category offered a mixture of traditional and modern attributes as the basis of their leadership preference. In terms of the age variable, then, the revolutionary regime could be encouraged by the fact that support for leaders possessing modernizing values was by far the strongest among the younger segments of the population, a fact that suggests that the most entrenched opposition to modernization should pass with time.

Far more striking were the differences in the support levels for leaders possessing traditional (ascriptive) attributes that emerged on the basis of urbanization ($G = 0.345$) and education ($G = 0.478$). Among the bedouins, the least sedentary segment of Libyan society, 60 percent of the respondents cited traditional attributes as the basis of their selection of the individuals best able to manage the village. This percentage dropped to 36 percent among rural villagers and to 29 percent among the more urbanized villagers. Preference for the modern attributes followed an inverse pattern, with only 12 percent of the bedouins citing modernizing attributes, as opposed to 26 percent of the rural villagers, and 34 percent of the semiurban villagers. Bedouins were also the least likely to offer a mixture of modern and traditional attributes as the basis of their support (29 percent). The corresponding figure for both the rural and semiurban villages was 38 percent.

Turning to education, the data presented in Table 5-2 provides a graphic illustration of the erosion of support for leaders possessing traditional attributes that has accompanied stepwise increases in the education level of rural Libyans. Among respondents with no formal education, support for leaders possessing traditional attributes exceeded 55 percent, a figure that dropped to 42 percent among respondents with primary education, and to 15 to 12 percent among respondents possessing vocational or secondary educations. No respondents

Table 5-2
Education and Declining Support for Traditional Elites

Leadership Attributes Preferred	Education Level				
	None	Primary	Preparatory	Vocational	College
Traditional	65.4%	55.3%	31.8%	22.2%	0%
Transitional	28.4	36.8	40.9	38.9	33.3
Modern	6.2	7.9	27.3	38.9	66.7
	100.0%	100.0%	100.0%	100.0%	100.0%
n	242	163	48	108	15
(Total: n = 576)	($G = 0.477$)				

possessing a college education offered traditional attributes as the basis of their support for the individual they felt best qualified to govern the village. Conversely, 72 percent of the college educated respondents gave their support to leaders possessing modernizing attributes, a figure that dropped to 55 percent and 42 percent among respondents possessing secondary or vocational educations, and to 17 percent among respondents passing primary education. Only 12 percent of the respondents lacking any form of formal education cited modernizing attributes as important factors in evaluating leadership preference.

Just as preferences for leaders possessing traditional attributes was strongest among the older, more rural, and less educated respondents, it was also the strongest among the most religious respondents and those respondents manifesting the most intense attachments to their tribe. Among extremely religious individuals, for example, 57 percent preferred traditional leadership attributes as opposed to 17 percent indicating support for modernizing values. The remainder of the extremely religious respondents cited a mixture of modern and traditional values as the basis of their leadership preferences. Mildly religious respondents, by contrast, cited traditional modern and mixed traditional/modern attributes in roughly equal proportions. Percentage distributions for tribal attachment item followed the same basic pattern.

Assuming that Libya's traditional local elites are sensitive to shifts in the locus of their support — an assumption unanimously supported by informal discussions with traditional and modernizing leaders alike — one would, indeed, expect them to view modernization programs of the RCC with severe skepticism if not open hostility. This would particularly appear to be the case in reference to programs relating to mass education or intensified media exposure. Further, the fact that support for traditional elites was also found to correlate with intensity of tribal attachment and the intensity of religious belief would suggest that traditional elites would be reluctant to champion causes that were unpopular among their supporters.

Tradition and Change among Local Elites

Up to this point, the analysis has indicated that the majority of the population studied continued to direct their primary loyalties toward the traditional local elites and that the ability of the traditional local elites to retain the loyalty of the masses rested upon such ascriptive attributes as religious piety, lineage, and the possession of traditional wisdom.

This brings the discussion to an analysis of the extent to which Libya's traditional leaders were predisposed for or against rapid social and economic change. If the data suggest that they are not unalterably opposed to change one would be tempted to suggest that they be reincorporated into the development process. This point is also of major theoretical interest, for, as noted earlier, most development theorists accept Colonel Qadafi's assumption that traditional elites are unalterably opposed to change.

In examining the receptivity of traditional elites to change, the study focused on four areas of elites' behavior: (1) general predisposition toward change; (2) overt manifestations of innovative behavior in reference to recognizing and solving their community's problems; (3) responsiveness to government initiated economic development programs; and (4) willingness to work with modernizing leaders and new institutional structures designed to accelerate economic, social, and political development.

Our effort to gauge the responsiveness of the traditional elites to economic modernization began with a battery of three questions designed to measure general attitudinal predispositions toward innovation and change. In line with Colonel Qadafi, we hypothesized that the general predispositions of the traditional elites would be opposed to change.

The results presented in Table 5-3 indicate that the general attitudes of the traditional leaders were strongly predisposed against innovation and change.

To elaborate on this theme and to ascertain their awareness of the fundamental social and economic problems besetting their villages, the traditional elites were next asked to identify those areas of village life in greatest need of improvement. Their responses were then compared with assessments of village needs provided by technical experts.

The results of this stage of the inquiry (Table 5-4) fell roughly into three groups. On items 1 through 4, relating to the need for long-term economic growth and requiring a substantial reordering of existing patterns of production, virtually no congruence existed between the views of the traditional elites and those of the government planners. On items 5 through 9, relating to community services, approximately 50 percent congruence existed between the views of the traditional elites and those of the technical experts. Finally, on items 10 through 13, relating to immediate and tangible needs, the views of the two groups were nearly identical. The lack of perceived need for welfare reflects the success of the government's program to eliminate hunger. Underemployment,

Table 5-3
Change Predispositions among Rural Libyan Elites

($n = 10$)	SA	A	D	SD
One should be concerned with what he has rather than what he can get.	1	9	0	0
Action should be delayed until one is sure of the desired results.	1	8	1	0
Change is desirable for itself.	1	1	8	0

Table 5-4
Contrasting Perceptions of Community Needs

Community Needs as Perceived by Traditional Leaders and Government Experts	Evaluation by Traditional Leaders (n = 10)		Evaluation by Experts (n = 10)	
	Inadequate	Adequate	Inadequate	Adequate
1. Workers' productivity	1	9	10	0
2. Distribution of resources	3	7	8	2
3. Agricultural growth	3	7	8	2
4. Popular support for development	2	8	10	0
5. Commercial development	0	10	5	5
6. Housing problems	2	8	8	2
7. Transportation/communications	4	6	8	2
8. Utilities (water, sewage)	6	4	10	0
9. Education/culture	3	7	7	3
10. Health and medicine	5	5	8	2
11. Technical skills	9	1	10	0
12. Social welfare	0	10	0	10
13. Underemployment	8	2	10	0

too, is a matter of direct personal importance to virtually all rural Libyans, one that long predates recent government concern with economic development.

The traditional elites, then, manifested little awareness of concern for the fundamental areas of long-term economic growth. They were far more aware of the need for more social services, an area of development financed solely by the central government and that required only minor alterations in existing life-styles. Even in this area, however, the enthusiasm of the traditional leaders was mixed.

Finding little predisposition toward innovation or change among the traditional elites surveyed, the interviewers next sought to measure overt hostility toward economic and social development.

Responses to the economic and social development items listed in Table 5-5 reflect a positive if somewhat ambivalent attitude toward economic development. As long as the questions spoke of development in the abstract and posed no immediate threat to the status quo, they were overwhelmingly supported by the traditional elites. Particularly evident during this stage of the interview process was the feeling that the traditional leaders were far less hostile to the prospects of economic and social modernization than to the prospect of further political modernization.

This fact was made abundantly clear in the responses to the interview items designed to measure the willingness of traditional elites to work through and cooperate with the new institutional frameworks established by the revolutionary government.

In this regard the interview schedules examined the willingness of the

Table 5-5
Receptivity of Traditional Rural Elites to the Value of Economic and Social Development

	SA	A	D	SD	(n = 10)
1. Achieving a higher standard of living is crucial to my village.	2	8	0	0	
2. Economic development is essential to further public satisfaction and welfare.	1	7	2	0	
3. Economic development should not be pursued if it means hardship for the people.	1	6	3	0	
4. Present generations are not obliged to worry about the resources of future generations.	0	0	8	2	
5. People should not be forced to contribute to the long range development of the community.	0	4	6	0	
6. Citizens must develop a greater interest in economic development.	1	8	1	0	
7. Formal education is of little help in real life.	0	1	9	0	
8. Adult education provides a great service to the community.	0	3	7	0	

traditional elites to work through or consult with the leaders of the Arab Socialist Union, a mass-based political organization established by the Revolutionary Council in an effort to establish closer ties with the masses. The interviews also stressed the attitudes of the traditional elites toward the new local officials appointed by the central government.

Responses to the cooperation items listed in Table 5-6 require no interpretation. The hostility of the traditional elites to modernizing institutions and officials was direct and explicit. Traditional elites often referred to the modernizing leaders as "young kids" and to the ASU as "kids' game." Items not cited also indicated that the hostility of the traditional leaders to their modernizing counterparts extended to virtually all areas of local administration.

In sum, then, the traditional elites showed little inclination toward innovation or development either in terms of attitudinal predispositions or in terms of perceiving innovative ways of improving the life of their villages. They were not, however, hostile to the abstract concept of change or to the desire to see the quality of life in their villages improved. They simply did not think in change-related or innovative terms. Their resistance to political change was adamant.

Table 5-6
Attitudes of Traditional Rural Elites toward Modernizing Administrators

	Yes	No	Nonresponse	(n = 10)
1. Would you consult with leaders of the local ASU in reference to community development?	1	9	–	
2. Would you consult with national leaders of the ASU to promote community development?	1	9	–	
3. Local government is staffed by competent men.	1	8	1	
4. Public officials are concerned with bettering the community.	0	10	–	

Summary and Conclusions

Having provided an empirical profile of Libya's traditional rural elite, ascertained their attitudinal predispositions toward social and economic change, and examined the bases of their popular support, we are now in a position to suggest some tentative conclusions concerning the question of whether the background, predispositions, and support base of traditional elites places them in a position of unalterable hostility to programs of rapid economic and social change. This question, as noted in the introduction, possesses both theoretical and applied relevance. In theoretical terms, the study provides an empirical examination of the assumption made by most development theorists that traditional elites are unalterably opposed to rapid social and economic change. In applied terms, the study has attempted to ascertain whether the RCC could markedly facilitate its goal of rapid economic and social development by co-opting traditional rural elites into the modernization process. The following points would seem particularly relevant to this query:

1. Without exception, the traditional elites studied owed their status, wealth, and position to the existence of a tribal/family-based theocracy. Changes in the status of the tribe and the social and religious traditions upon which tribal authority is based would seem to result in the erosion of their authority.
2. All the traditional rural elites studied manifested a strong attachment to their tribes and to their religious heritage. They manifested intense hostility to new political institutions such as the ASU.
3. Because of their background characteristics and their strong tribal and

religious attachments, the traditional rural elites found it difficult to conceptualize village problems in change-oriented terms. Their solutions overwhelmingly tended to be the solutions of the past.

4. While predisposed against change and resisting projects that directly threatened their position, the traditional elites were not unreceptive to increased social services financed by the central government. They were, however, intensely hostile toward the modernizing administrators appointed by the RCC and deeply resented their own removal from the reform process. They similarly resented the creation of the Arab Socialist Union and, in particular, its local officials.

5. Traditional rural elites were listed as the individuals best suited to rule their villages by more than 67 percent of the respondents. This indicates that their support remains intact in spite of strenuous government efforts to undermine their authority and that they could, if they so desired, serve as a potent force in the RCC's effort to mobilize Libya's predominantly rural populations toward projects of socioeconomic development.

6. Support for the traditional rural elites was by far the strongest among the older, least educated, and less urbanized respondents. The same respondents also manifested the strongest levels of tribal and religious attachment. The traditional elites are thus reinforced in their opposition to change by the values of their supporters. By the same token, the attachment of their supporters to the ways of the past would appear to further constrain traditional elites from pursuing projects which conflict with traditional norms.

In sum, the results support the hypothesis that the traditional rural elites are inimical to the pursuit of rapid social, economic, and political change.

Somewhat less clear is whether the traditional rural elites would be opposed to moderate social and economic changes instituted under their leadership. It will be recalled that the strongest opposition of the traditional rural elites to RCC modernization programs was in the areas of administrative reorganization and social planning. While not conceptualizing village problems in innovative terms, they were not unalterably opposed to increased social services or to technological changes related to immediate village needs. At the same time, the intense hostility of the traditional elites to the ASU and to the modernizing administrators raises serious questions as to just how far the traditional rural elites could realistically be incorporated into the development process.

However, the substantial popular support that continues to accrue to the traditional rural elites and the extreme difficulty experienced by the RCC in attempting to penetrate the rural masses suggests that the RCC has little to lose by attempting to placate the traditional rural elites by co-opting them into the development process to the greatest extent possible, at least until such time as ongoing reform programs have made the rural populations more receptive to the style of more technologically oriented administrators.

Notes

1. Mu'ammar El-Qathafi, *Discourses* (Adam Publishers, 1975).
2. International Bank for Reconstruction and Development, *The Economic Development of Libya* (Baltimore: John Hopkins University Press, 1960).

John Wright, *Libya* (New York: Frederick A. Praeger, Publishers, 1969).

Elizabeth R. Hayford, "The Politics of the Kingdom of Libya in Historical Perspective," (Tufts University, 1971).

Salaheddin Salem Hasan, "The Genesis of the Political Leadership of Libya 1952-1969: Historical Origins and Development of its Component Elements" (The George Washington University, 1973).

3. Gabriel A. Almond and Sidney Verba, *Civic Culture* (Boston: Little, Brown, 1963).

Talcott Parsons, *Structure of Social Action* (Glencoe, Ill.: The Free Press, 1949).

Gideon Sjorberg, "The Rural-Urban Dimension in Preindustrial, Transitional, and Industrial Societies," in Robert E. L. Faris, ed., *Handbook of Modern Sociology* (Chicago: Rand McNally, 1964), pp. 127-159.

Ferdinand Tonnies, *Community and Society Gemeinschaft and Geselschaft.* Translated and edited by C. P. Loomis (East Lansing: Michigan State University Press, 1947).

4. F. X. Sutton, "Social Theory and Comparative Politics," in Harry Eckstein and David E. Apter, eds., *Comparative Politics* (Glencoe, Ill.: The Free Press, 1963), pp. 67-82.

Gideon Sjoberg, "Folk and Feudal Societies," *American Journal of Sociology* 58 (November 1952): 231-39; Hehmet Beqiraj, *Peasantry in Revolution* (Ithaca, N.Y.: Cornell University Press, 1966).

5. Everett E. Hagen, *On the Theory of Social Change* (Homewood, Ill.: Dorsey Press, 1962), pp. 68-69, 124-157.

John C. McKinney, *Constructive Typology and Social Theory* (New York: Appleton-Century-Crofts, 1966).

Helio Jaquaribe, *Political Development: A General Theory and a Latin American Case Study* (New York: Harper & Row, 1973).

6. W. W. Rostow, *The Process of Economic Growth*, 2nd ed. (New York: W. W. Norton, 1952, 1962) p. 307. With permission of publisher.

Joseph A. Kahl, *The Measurement of Modernism: A Study of Values in Brazil and Mexico*, Latin American Monographs, no. 12 (Austin, Tex.: Institute of Latin American Studies, University of Texas, 1968); David Horton Smith and Alex Inkeles, "The OM scale: A Comparative Socio-Psychological Measure of Individual Modernity," *Sociometry* 29 (December 1966): 353-77.

Numerous examples of this situation can be found in Kalman H. Silvert, ed., *Expectant Peoples* (New York: Random House, 1963), Kuswin Nair, *Blossoms in the Dust* (London: C. Duckworth, 1961); George Dalton, ed.,

Economic Development and Social Change: The Modernization of Village Communities (Garden City, N.Y.: The Natural History Press, 1971).

Samuel P. Huntington, *Political Order in Changing Societies* (New Haven: Yale University Press, 1968).

7. Lloyd I. Rudolph and Susanne Hoeber Rudolph, *The Modernity of Tradition* (Chicago: University of Chicago Press, 1967).

8. Willis D. Hawley and Frederick M. Wirt, eds., *The Search for Community Power*, (Englewood Cliffs, N.J.: Prentice-Hall, 1968).

Michael Aiken and Paul E. Mott, eds., *The Structure of Community Power* (New York: Random, 1970).

6

Leadership, Institutionalization, and Mass Participation in Libya
Omar I. El Fathaly and *Richard Chackerian*

Samuel Huntington has suggested that in most developing areas the forces of social change have outrun institutional reforms, and that, as a consequence, institutional frameworks fail to keep pace with the conditions of their environment. Perhaps an exception to this rule is the rapidly changing set of formal institutions that are the product of the September 1, 1969, Libyan revolution. The rapid changes that have characterized Libya since 1969 provide a unique opportunity to study how a complex set of institutional transitions have drastically altered the pattern of local leadership in ways that are designed to be supportive of mass participation, mobilization, and development in Libya.

The purposes of this chapter are to (1) describe the changes in institutional arrangements, (2) describe the changes in leadership that have paralleled the institutional changes, and (3) ask how these changes in leadership and institutions are likely to impact the capacity of local leadership to encourage mass participation and to channel that participation to developmental goals.

A basic assumption of our research is that the effectiveness of institutions depends on the nature of the relationship between institutional leaders and the mass public on the one hand and the sympathy of institutional leaders with developmental goals on the other. Mass mobilization and participation depend at least on the capacity of the leadership to communicate to the mass public that there is congruence between the public's perception of values and the values which are projected by the behavior of the leadership. A fact that complicates this relationship in Libya, and in other developing countries, is that, in addition to having leadership that can mobilize and be sympathetic to development, it is necessary to cope with and change the traditionalism of both the local leadership and the mass public which definitionally is hostile to change. In a sense, then, the test of institutions in these developing countries is their ability to recruit initially to positions of institutional leadership those whose values and sensitivities are both traditional and modern, and later to change so as to reduce increasingly traditional influences. Then overriding element in the likely effectiveness of institutional arrangements is their capacity to change local leadership as the public moves from traditional to more modern views of public involvement.

This chapter was presented as a paper at the Tenth Annual Meeting of the Middle East Studies Association, Los Angeles, California, November 10-13, 1976.

Research Procedures

Research procedures employed in this chapter are described in Chapter 1.

Modernizing Leaders, Institutions, and the Public

The revolutionary leadership recognized that the traditional leaders help great influence over the public and that they were resistant to developmental change. In October 1969, traditional leaders were purged from local government positions and were replaced, through appointment, with "modernizing" leaders. In addition, the tribal system was legally dismantled and a single political organization, the Arab Socialist Union (ASU), was created in June 1971 to fill the void.

The legal status of tribes was destroyed by dividing tribal areas into zones crossing old tribal boundaries, combining parts of different tribes within one zone. Leadership also was radically changed because sheikhs, whose positions were inherited or selected on ascriptive bases, were replaced by zone administrators selected on the basis of skills and education. Such strategies were designed to minimize tribal and regional identification, but also to bring the mass public into closer touch with the regime and to provide leadership, technical skills, and attitudes necessary for development.

The modernizing leaders in Libya have been largely representative of a new generation of administrators in similar developing countries whose stress on administrative reform is still the predominant approach to modernization and development. The literature on the Middle East generally describes these new administrators as follows: (1) they have been mainly of middle-class economic origins and background, rather than upper-class, with formal education being more important for appointment than family preferment; (2) they are younger; (3) they are more likely to support and be ideologically committed to development goals; (4) they have tended to be less corrupt than their predecessors; and (5) they have been more professional and more aware of modern "administrative science."[1] Most of these characteristics fit the attributes of the modernizing leaders in Zavia province. They have tended to come from humble backgrounds. In terms of socioeconomic status, 74 percent are the sons of farmers and 9 percent of shopkeepers. Forty-five percent considered their families to be middle class, 25 percent as lower class, and 21 percent as upper-middle class, while none belonged to the upper class.

Their average age was thirty-eight years, and for the mayors and deputy mayors thirty-five, a very young age in the Libyan context to assume such a responsible position.

The modernizing leaders' educational level was substantially higher than that of the traditional officials who had occupied local government positions.

Thirty-three percent obtained college degrees, 25 percent graduated from vocational training, and the rest had completed primary or preparatory school. Excluding municipal department directors, college graduates constituted 73 percent of the sample. Consistent with the relatively high educational level of the modernizers, they are heavily exposed to all types of mass media, much more so than traditional leaders. Table 6-1 shows the distribution of this exposure.

In terms of their social and religious characteristics, the modernizers are transitional in that they profess to be very religious (70 percent) but they do not show the piety of traditional leaders, only 17 percent praying daily and 15 percent having made the pilgrimage to Mecca. The modernizing leaders' tribal credentials were moderate to poor. The majority reported that they belonged to tribes, but their attachment to or pride taken in their tribes was moderate. The transitional character of modernizers is also evident in their placing the education of the young (30 percent), *and* conflict avoidance (30 percent) as top policy priorities. Public participation was seen as a top priority by only 5 percent of the modernizers.

The evidence then suggests that the modernizing leaders increased the technical capacity of the regime to respond to the requirements of development, but because of their socioeconomic origins, and attitudes towards the centrality of change and participation, were not likely to be successful modernizers of the public.

The public correctly understands the modernizers' lack of concern for public participation and tends to generalize this understanding to a negative perception of them as community leaders. For example, the public sample was asked several questions on how receptive the mayor was to their participation. The results indicate a substantial feeling of official nonresponsiveness (see Table 6-2).

In addition to the public feeling that mayors did not encourage their participation, the evidence also suggests an absence of general support. When asked if they would vote for the mayors, 58 percent of the public answered no. Of 576 respondents, 71 percent thought the majority of the community would not vote for the mayors, and finally, when asked if the mayors were considered the most influential, respected, trusted, and popular leaders in the community, 60 percent answered no. These findings indicate that the public would not turn to the modernizing leadership in the event they were given the chance to make that decision. In retrospect, it seems clear that it was the administrative-technical mission rather than public involvement and mobilization that was seen by the modernizers as their primary function.

The Arab Socialist Union was created as the primary link between the mass public and the government. It was hoped that it would "provide a pervasive network capable of observing and reporting throughout the society."[2] The ASU, through its structure, was to co-opt the masses where they could

Table 6-1
Modernizing Leaders' Exposure to Media

Frequency of Exposure	Every Day		Few Times a Week		Once a Week		Once a Month		Few Times a Month	
	No.	Percentage	No.	Percentage	No.	Percentage	No.	Percentage	No.	Percentage
Newspaper	(7)	29	(3)	13	(3)	13	(8)	33	(3)	13
Television	(18)	75	(4)	17	(1)	4	(1)	4	(0)	—
Radio	(22)	92	(1)	4	(1)	4	(0)	—	(0)	—

n = 24

Table 6-2
Public Perception of Mayors' Attitudes toward Community Participation

	Agree		Disagree	
	No.	Percentage	No.	Percentage
1. Mayors listen to citizens' opinions.	(272)	48	(297)	52
2. Mayors ask for citizens' opinions.	(242)	43	(327)	57
3. Mayors discuss community problems and programs with public.	(242)	43	(328)	57
4. Mayors encourage public to participate.	(238)	42	(326)	58

$N = 576$

be motivated to participate, and be politicized and mobilized for developmental goals. As Qadafi declared in his address on June 11, 1971 (the official date establishing the ASU), "The ASU will bring about collaboration among the popular working classes, liquidate differences, if any, between the classes, realize real democracy, and unite with the revolution against one-class dictatorship."[3] Although we shall have more to say about the ASU later, it is clear that in this early period it failed in its mobilization and participation roles for several reasons, including: (1) negative preconceptions based on the Egyptian counterpart, (2) a complex organizational structure which confused the public, (3) a failure to understand the traditionalism of the public and the central role of traditional leaders in the development of public perceptions, and (4) a failure to coordinate with the new modernizing local officials.

Three years after the 1969 revolution, the Revolutionary Command Council (RCC) began to express dissatisfaction with their strategy for institutional change. While the notion of administrative expertise had been established, they realized that both the ASU and the new local leadership had failed to create a link of solidarity between the masses and local governmental institutions. It was hoped by the revolutionary regime that these institutional changes would have broken the congruence between the public and their traditional leaders and destroy public trust and loyalty to traditional institutions and leaders. But the power of the traditional leaders, resting in part, as it did, on the public's loyalty to tradition, was far stronger than the new leadership anticipated. The RCC responded to these failures by initiating the Popular Revolution, which was announced by Qadafi on April 15, 1973.

Popular Committee Leadership, Institutions, and the Public

Formally, the Popular Revolution had five major objectives: (1) to suspend all laws currently enforced because of their "reactionary" character; (2) to purge the country of all people who are politically "sick." This applied to people who "preach communism and capitalism as well as Muslim Brethren if they engage in clandestine activities"; (3) to distribute arms to the people (the popular militia) to be used against the people's enemies from within and without; (4) to start a cultural revolution; and (5) to launch an administrative revolution.[4]

Qadafi explained, "Those . . . who have formed a barrier between the revolution and the masses . . . this bourgeois class, the bureaucrats . . . The masses must destroy bureaucracy and destroy barriers." He continued, "If the interests of the people are going to be lost for the sake of the government, down with the government and long live the people."[5]

The institutional cornerstone of the Popular Revolution was the popular committees, bodies elected directly by the people. Qadafi declared "people everywhere should set up people's committees in every village, city, faculty, institute, school, harbor, airport, and popular organization . . . in order to put into implementation the five-point program."[6] Direct popular elections were restricted to zones, more general levels of representation being achieved by the election of representatives from the membership of zone committees to muncipal and provincial committees. Direct elections were also held in public corporations and government bureaucracies, with representatives from each of these units being sent to the muncipal and provincial committees. The electors in municipal and provincial elections were the members of the zone committees.

The establishment of the popular committees signaled the abolition of the local government modernizing structures and a reduction in the power position of modernizing officials. Local administrative functions were transferred to the popular committees, with the chairman of the municipal and provincial popular committees becoming, respectively, the chief administrative official for the municipality and the province.

The popular committees, in addition to their administrative responsibility, were given full legislative authority in what might be called, broadly, service functions. Decisions about health clinics, minor roads, schools, sewage, water, parks, social clubs, and so on, were within the policy domain of these municipal level committees. The provincial committees were given responsibility in many of the same functions, but tended to have determinative roles where the scope of the function crossed municipal boundaries. For example, some of the more important provincial concerns are major highways, hospitals, vocational training centers, major electric plants, and agricultural development.

The popular committee approach formally required, for the first time, popular involvement in the selection of local leaders and allowed popular involvement in local policymaking processes. It was clearly the intention of the RCC to provide an opportunity for the public to increase their political experience through participation and to concentrate public attention on issues concerning their immediate community. It was hoped also that popular committees would function as a mobilizing agent and source of organized support for the government, its programs, and its policies. These changes in the institutional structure had a marked impact on the nature of local leadership.

Of the sixty popular committee members interviewed, the majority were farmers, workers, and government employees. Almost all of them were born, raised, and had lived in the same area. Sixty-three percent of this group were rural, and the rest were divided equally between bedouin and urban populations. Seventy-four percent were less than forty years old, 15 percent belonged to the forty to sixty age group, and the rest were sixty and over. The average educational level of the popular committee members was less than the modernizing leaders but higher than both public and traditional leaders. This comparison is shown in Table 6-3.

The popular committee members showed less tribal affiliation, tribal attachment, or pride than the other subsamples. Generally, the popular committee members belonged to less prestigious families and tribes, and their election was not based upon the support from their tribes, but rather upon their relationships with the community and their immediate associates.

The majority of the popular committee members, 77 percent, were of the middle class, and their average income, although higher than the public average, was much less than those of both modernizers and traditionals.

In the area of religion, the distribution of popular committee responses is only slightly different from that of the public, falling midway between the modernizing and traditional leaders.

In terms of their informational and education status, popular committees are on the average midway between the modernizers and traditional leaders, being distinctly less educated that the modernizers but more educated and exposed to the media than traditional leaders.

The popular committees were closer than traditional leaders to the public in their evaluation of public programs and municipal officials and in their support of popular participation (see Table 6-4).

As significant as their hostility to the modernizing administrators and perhaps also hostility to traditional leaders are the relatively close contacts with the ASU. Although they exhibited generally lower levels of interaction within their community, they, of all subsamples, had the highest interaction rate with the ASU, an institution that was to be revitalized and integrated with popular committees in the latest wave of institutional change.

As we shall show, the Popular Revolution did not resolve some of the central problems of mobilization, participation, and development; but some substantial gains were made. Popular committees represented a local leadership

Table 6-3
Educational Levels of Traditional Leaders, Public, Popular Committee Members, and the Modernizing Leaders

	Traditional Leaders		Public		Popular Committees		Modernizing Leaders	
	No.	Percentage	No.	Percentage	No.	Percentage	No.	Percentage
None	(0)	—	(242)	42	(8)	13	(0)	—
Preprimary and primary	(7)	70	(163)	28	(30)	50	(8)	33
Preparatory, secondary, and vocational	(2)	20	(156)	27	(21)	35	(8)	33
College	(1)	10	(15)	3	(1)	2	(8)	33

Table 6-4
Evaluations of the Modernizers by Popular Committee Members

Leadership Qualities	Evaluations	
	Percentage Agreeing	Percentage Disagreeing
Modernizing leaders are capable men	39.0	61.0
Trusted, respected by public	46.7	53.3
Interested in public welfare	18.6	81.4
Successful	25.9	74.1
Mayor listens to community opinion	23.7	76.3
Asks for citizens' opinions	10.2	89.8
Discusses community problems with public	20.3	79.7
Encourages public participation	10.3	89.7
Represents the ideal leadership	23.7	76.3
Accepted by majority	25.0	75.0

$N = 60$

which in cultural and policy terms was closer to the mass public than the modernizers, yet unlike traditional leaders they were sympathetic to popular participation. These changes in leadership, together with the right of popular election and the formal subordination of municipal officials to strictly administrative roles, undoubtedly has weakened the traditional leaders' hold on the mass public and reduced the influence of expertise by the modernizers.

Qadafi, in spite of these changes, continued to express dissatisfaction, but increasingly it focused not on political participation or expertise in the bureaucracy but on popular mobilization. Some of the difficulty in developing a capacity for mass mobilization seemed to be rooted in the conflict that developed between the ASU and the popular committees over which was the central institution for popular mobilization. This factor and others contributed to Qadafi's dissatisfaction with popular committees and to yet a third major set of institutional changes to encourage public mobilization.

The People's Congress, Workers' Unions, ASU Leadership, and the Public

The basic objectives in this third stage of reform were to insure that popular committees and the ASU would more closely coordinate their activities and reduce the conflict and competition that sometimes characterized their relations, and to co-opt workers' unions directly into an integrated participatory apparatus. These objectives required some shifting of functions and authority between the popular committees and the ASU as well as increasing the institutional integration of popular committees, the ASU, and the unions.

More specifically, on September 1, 1975, Qadafi declared that zones and direct popular election to zone committees would be retained. Also, following the substance of the older model, zone committees in a district (which are similar in geographic scope to municipalities) were to elect from their membership a "people's basic congress." At this point, however, there is a basic departure from the older popular committee model in that the people's basic congress elects from its members a popular committee whose functions are formally restricted to administration. Political authority is delegated to the district ASU, the leadership of which is elected from the membership of the people's basic congress. The strengthened position of the ASU is also indicated by the requirement that the chairman of the people's basic congress must be a representative from the ASU.

In addition, all workers were required to join appropriate occupationally defined unions and to elect from their membership leaders and representatives to district-level unions. The use of occupational groups as units of representation was substituted for the earlier dependence on work places as units of representation.

The new representational institution at the national level is the People's General Congress. The chairmen and assistant chairmen of all district popular committees and district ASUs are automatically delegates to the General Congress. In addition, district union leaders and their deputies are entitled to be delegates to the General Congress.

The General Congress, in its annual sessions, is the major arena in which the plans and programs of the RCC and those developed at the district level are discussed and ratified, ratification implying the responsibility of unions, the ASU, and popular committees for implementation. (See Appendix A).

Much to the surprise of most Libyans, the RCC and the Cabinet transmitted all major government plans and policies for review and authorization by the General Congress. The most significant items on the agenda were the 1976 general budget (administrative) and the 1976-1980 development budget, as well as major domestic and foreign policy items. In Qadafi's October 7, 1976, speech, he further expanded the authority of the People's General Congress by allocating to them the authority to appoint and dismiss cabinet members, issue laws, and determine foreign policy.

The ASU has been strengthened considerably in this latest series of institutional changes; therefore it is important to review some of their more important characteristics, recognizing that our data are limited by a small sample.

Conclusion

Changes in formal institutions and leaders which have taken place in Libya since 1969 are of phenomenal proportions by Western standards. While it is much too early to assess the ultimate effectiveness of these changes, there are the appearances of complex yet logically consistent strategy of institutional development and differentiation.

The problems to which these changes have been addressed are fairly clear: (1) encourage mass participation and mobilization, (2) increase the technical response capacity of governmental institutions, and (3) channel participation and governmental response to support regime development goals.

The responses to these problems initially were primitive in the sense that institutional arrangements remained unchanged from traditional forms of local government, although modernizing administrators were appointed to positions of formal leadership. The modernizers, however, were not interested in public participation and the public "knew it." The practical effect of this official indifference was to allow traditional leaders to maintain their hold on the traditional public.

One is tempted to hypothesize that the initial dependence on the old structure of local government could not have worked because it was insufficiently differentiated. The modernizing administrators were committed, basically, to technical-administrative problems, and perhaps found questions of mobilization and participation inconsistent with the neater logic of the administrative-technical world. The old structure simply did not provide institutional protection of the "core technologies" which undoubtedly would have been threatened if mass participation had been encouraged. This is not to suggest that modernizers were not aware of the importance of the local political environment, but only that by training and background they were more dependent on traditional leaders than the mass public.

The popular committees implied a similar institutional oversimplification, but in the opposite direction. In this case, the pendulum swung to a heavy emphasis on popular participation and mobilization. This change, however, was significant for two reasons. First, it strengthened the principle of local elections. Second, it significantly changed the character of local leadership. The new leaders were clearly more "of the people" in that their class origins were more humble than both modernizers and traditionals; they supported popular participation and held only moderate to weak attachments to traditional values. As central was the shift from traditional leaders as a source of support to the membership of the ASU. The vesting of authority in the hands of popular committees was the first successful step toward isolating traditional leaders from their loyal public. The strategy of isolation, however, did not fully develop until the people's congresses were instituted.

The highly differentiated congress structure, with popular committees acting as administrative agents and the ASU acting as "legislative" agents, will, perhaps, provide the institutional differentiation required to deal with the problems of participation, mobilization, and technical capacity and support of development goals. The electoral and authority relationships are plausible, but the history of institutional development has created the necessary social and attitudinal differentiation among local leadership. This differentiation may allow the enactment of functions which in a single organization are to some extent incompatible. In addition, the congress structure provides an integrative framework which encourages participation and mobilization at the bottom and substantial control by the regime at the top. Another implication of this elaboration of functions and structures is that it is likely to leave traditional leaders without functions and therefore without popular following.

Notes

1. James Bill and Carl Leiden, *The Middle East: Politics and Power* (Boston: Allyn and Bacon, 1974), pp. 186-88.
2. Richard Nyrop, *Area Handbook for Libya* (Washington, D.C.: U.S. Government Printing Office, 1973), p. 171.
3. Ibid.
4. George Lenczowski, "Popular Revolution in Libya," *Current History* (February 1974), p. 57.
5. Ibid.
6. Ibid., p. 59.

Part III

7

From Bureaucratic to Open Systems: Models of Development Administration
Richard Chackerian

The Libyan revolutionary leaders have instituted a series of institutional changes which are hoped will dramatically change the basic conditions of life. We have in the previous chapters described some of the institutional and attitudinal aspects of these changes, but we have not systematically meshed the facts of the Libyan case with existing models of development administration. This effort is made difficult by the fact that the impacts of the institutional changes in Libya are yet to be described. The question that seems appropriate under these circumstances is, With which models of development are the changes in Libya consistent? The procedure will be to review existing models of development administration, suggest how these models might be informed by the open-systems literature, and, finally, show how this revised open-systems approach is more useful for understanding the Libyan case than more traditional perspectives.

The Struggle to Preserve Bureaucracy as a Model of Development Administration

In 1966, Ferrel Heady could say, in what became a widely read textbook in comparative administration, "By far the most prominent and promising middle-range model available for comparative studies in administration is the bureaucratic one, based upon the ideal-type model of bureaucracy as formulated by Max Weber...."[1] The major categories of analysis, given a bureaucratic perspective are those of (1) hierarchy of formal authority and (2) differentiation or specialization of the task structure within the structure of authority. Other characteristics can be and have been discussed as essential, such as merit or competence of position incumbents, but these are essentially derivative of the logic of hierarchy and specialization. Specialization of the task structure is said to provide the efficiencies and economies that less specialized task structures cannot provide. Hierarchy is necessary because, as the level of task specialization increases, it becomes increasingly difficult to coordinate or integrate the task execution. Put otherwise, as specialization becomes more elaborate so also must strategies for the coordination of task execution, hierarchy being the strategy which is given the central place in bureaucratic approaches. While it may be obvious, it is important to note that the notion of integration or coordination necessarily implies some notion of goals. Coordination is determined and judged with regard to some well-agreed-upon purposes. Activity is judged to be coordinated or integrated only with regard to some purpose.

The early justifications for the focus on bureaucracy were both prescriptive and descriptive. Bureaucracy was regarded, in principle, as a universal phenomenon which made it a unit of analysis of widespread importance. Its universality had the technical advantage of allowing comparisons between cultures and nations. For example, Heady reported, "A necessary consequence of hierarchy and specialization in large-scale organization is an orderly arrangement of units into successively larger and more inclusive groupings. This process of departmentalization has occurred in a remarkably uniform wasy in countries that vary greatly in their political orientation and in other aspects of their administrative systems."[2] More important for these purposes is that bureaucracy was regarded as the major instrument for enhancing development of the Third World.

The efficiency and effectiveness of bureaucratic arrangements was assumed; analysis, description, and discussion centered around strategies for assuring that the ideals of the bureaucratic model might be fulfilled in particular settings. For example, Wallace S. Sayre[3] focuses on the variation between countries in how bureaucrats are chosen, their role in decision making, and how bureaucrats are to be governed. As Berger[4] has indicated, these questions are really about how individuals and groups within and outside the formal structure of bureaucracy respond to its formal requirements. They focus directly on administrative behavior rather than on the efficacy of the structural arrangements, recognizing of course that the behavioral concomitants of structure are important in its evaluation. The basic assumption of these analyses of bureaucratic behavior is that bureaucratic arrangements are probably effective, and that it is, therefore, important to see the extent to which actual behaviors in bureaucratic structures conform to expectations, that is, the extent to which the behaviors are themselves bureaucratic and therefore effective and efficient.

In retrospect, it seems obvious that bureaucratic structures are not likely to result in bureaucratic behavior in the developing countries. This conclusion is strongly implied in the early work by John Gaus on the "ecology of administration" and later and more specifically by Riggs. "Bureaucracies can be better understood if the surrounding conditions, influences and forces that shape them are identified and ranked to the extent possible in order of relative importance."[5] The ecological approach usually included some attempt to trace the relationship between social, economic, or political variables and the structural or behavioral characteristics of bureaucracy. Indeed, several attempts were made to classify social, economic, and political factors into models of environment and administration. Riggs's "fused," "diffracted," and "prismatic societies," the latter having a "sala" administration, were perhaps the most prominent typology. "Rates of political and bureaucratic growth are imbalanced in prismatic society; there the bureaucracy has the advantage in competition with political institutions, which might be better able to control the bureaucracy in diffracted societies, whether pluralistic or totalitarian. The weight of bureaucratic power in prismatic society tempts bureaucrats to interfere in the political process."[6] The sala model is also associated with such nonbureaucratic characteristics as inefficiency, unequal distribution of services, institutionalized corruption, neopotism, self-protectionism, and in general a gap between formal expectations and actual behavior.

In spite of the widespread recognition, then, that actual administrative behavior may be widely divergent from formal bureaucratic expectations, the bureaucratic model either implicitly or explicitly remains the normative standard for comparative empirical research and for administrative prescription.

Since the bureaucratic model provides normative standards for comparative research and prescription, and since there is a recognition that societal conditions in developing countries "compromise" bureaucratic behavior, it should not be surprising to find a literature that is concerned either with changing socioeconomic environmental conditions as precedent to administrative reform (bureaucratization) or is concerned with how to insulate administrative systems in developing countries from "dysfunctional" environmental influences.

The strategy of insulation is documented by Brian Loveman[7] in his discussion of the Comparative Administration Group (CAG). He notes the statement by Esman, a prominent member of the CAG, that

> To a number of scholars, including this writer, the emphasis on control of bureaucracy in the context of most of the developing countries is a misplaced priority, one that might seriously retard the rate of progress. We ought to be much more concerned with increasing the capacity of the bureaucracy to perform, and this we see as a function of greatly enhanced professional capability and operational autonomy rather than further controls.[8]

In the same article Loveman quotes Pye as saying that "in large measure the story of the Third World is one of countless efforts to create organizations by which resources can be effectively mobilized for achieving new objectives ... and that the acculturative process in the army tends to be focused on acquiring skills that are of particular value for economic development."[9]

What seemed to develop in the writings of comparative administration scholars was what Thompson later was to call the tendency of organizations to protect their core technology through leveling of environmental demands,[10] in this case the leveling being through the use of military skills.

Scholars, perhaps seeing the difficulty of building bureaucratic and technological capabilities or feeling that the military alternative to these problems was unacceptable, tended to translate the bureaucratic capability problem into more general strategies of economic capability. The hope was that once the economic conditions were right, social and eventually governmental-bureaucratic capability would develop. The advantage of this approach is that economic development would not only result in increased bureaucratic capability but also in liberal democracy. The argument made for these conclusions is that economic development creates an economic surplus which in turn reduces the severity of political competition. The institutionalization of civil rights and democratic procedures is then possible because the political struggle is not over matters of survival.[11] The economic surplus created by economic development also allows greater support of administrative professionalization.

In some respects the emphasis on economic development and professionalization is not greatly different from the administrative capability approach. However, the logic of economic development might be to promote professionalism first in the private sector, through large-scale industrial development projects, and only later in governmental bureaucracies.

The strength of the emphasis on the economic system is that it provides an open-systems view of administrative behavior. Once the economic system is modernized and made more productive, then public organizations would adapt to these professional norms and necessarily, in the long run, become more bureaucratized, effective, and efficient. The significance of these formulations for our purposes is that whether the model of administrative development is that of the economic development of that of those who emphasize bureaucratic behavior, the standard of evaluation is essentially Weberian.

It is particularly interesting that, for some who advocate bureaucratization and at the same time see the political and administrative institutions as subject to environmental influences, "absorbing mass demands" is a major concern. For example, Halpren defines development as "the relationship between the structural changes and demands set loose by the uncontrolled forces of transformation and the will and capacity of political authority to cope with these changes and demands."[12] While it may be overstating the case somewhat, he seems to fear the "uncontrolled forces of transformation" and to regretfully acknowledge the open nature of even the most rigid political and administrative systems. Thus the major concern is to develop institutions that can "absorb" mass demands, because if they cannot develop this capability, political and administrative instability is the likely result.

Huntington, one of the more sophisticated of these writers defined institutionalization in terms of "adaptability, complexity, autonomy, and coherence of its organizations and procedures." Huntington seems to have accepted the biological analogy as an appropriate normative standard for institutionalization and implicitly administrative organization. An institution from this perspective "is more nearly a natural product of social needs and pressures; a responsive, adaptive organism." This perspective is distinctive in that short-run, incremental, adaptive responses to day-to-day pressures are as important for institutional patterns as planned, comprehensively rational action.

Clearly the ecological and biological models of administrative organization emphasize the environment. Regardless, however, of whether the strategy of administrative response is adaptation or insulation, the presumed form of administrative capability is essentially bureaucratic. Consistent with bureaucratic models of administration is the common theme that increases in internal differentiation and autonomy will enhance the effectiveness of administrative units in responding to environmental challenges.

The Open-Systems Perspective: The Centrality of Exchange and Equifinality

Hass and Drabek[13] argue that while there is substantial convergence between open systems and biological perspectives such as Huntington's, the differences are substantial. Among the most important of these, for our purposes, is that rather than emphasizing adaptation, interaction or exchange with the environment in patterns of mutual influence are given greater prominence. This difference is particularly important for the development literature because it requires one to look not only at those institutional arrangements which make sense as adaptations to rising mass demands (strategies to absorb) but also to analyze the ways in which institutions and administrative organizations can *stimulate* mass participation in both administrative and policy processes. In certain programmatic areas, mass participation becomes a problem not because of its presence, but because of its absence. The organizational question is not simply how to initiate bureaucratic arrangements which will absorb environmental pressures, but also the pattern of arrangements that is needed to stimulate involvement. As we shall see, bureaucratic arrangements may be ill suited to this purpose, and that less specialized and hierarchical forms of organization may be much more appropriate. Indeed, the case can be made that the "strategy of insulation" from the environment is best served by bureaucratic arrangements. But even here there is the danger of being overly deterministic in the specification of administrative arrangements. This suggests another major strength of the open-systems perspective, namely the notion of equifinality.

Equifinality means that "the same final state (development) can be reached from different initial conditions and in different ways."[14] Variation in institutions and organizations is due not only to different environmental conditions and learning, but also to different ways of dealing with the "same problem."

Equifinality is a concept of great significance for the comparative administrative literature. It is noncontroversial, at least in retrospect, that there is usually more than one best way to organize. The more difficult questions arise when one begins to ask questions about the range of organizations that are appropriate to specific types of environmental conditions. This raises the question of how to conceptualize the organizational environments, since this must be accomplished before specification of exchanges with it are possible. Once the environment has been conceptualized, it is then possible to specify the types of administrative differentiation and coordination that are likely to be successful. It must be emphasized that normatively acceptable patterns of exchange, from the open-systems perspective, imply a variety of patterns of differentiation and coordination which may or may not coincide with the bureaucratic model.

Environments of Open Systems: Certainty and Stability

A useful conceptualization of environment has been developed by Lawrence and Lorsch[15] who emphasize the degree of certainty of information in the organizational environment which must be transmitted to the organization if its outputs to the environment are to be effective. Certainty is said to be low where the "causal linkages" in organizational technology are poorly understood, where the time between organizational outputs and feedback of impact results is relatively long, and relatedly where the relevant environment is thought to be undergoing rapid transformation. Recognizing that the particular conditions causing uncertainty are not exhausted by this list, they are all plausibly central. Lawrence and Lorsch found, among effective organizations, five measurable features that varied with the degree of environmental certainty and change:[16]

1. the degree of reliance on formalized rules and formal communication channels within the unit;
2. the time horizon of managers and professionals;
3. their orientation toward goals, etiher diffuse or concentrated;
4. their interpersonal style, either relationship or task-oriented; and
5. the degree of elaboration in integrative mechanisms.

In order to relate effectively to its environment, any organization must have reasonably accurate and timely information about the environment and especially about environmental changes. This is clearly an easier job if the environment is relatively stable. The job can be specified in a predetermined set of operating rules. The necessary messages can be handled through the traditional superior-subordinate channels, which may be few and constricted but are probably less subject to error and relatively inexpensive. Fairly short time horizons are usually adequate to take account of the reactions of such an environment . . . This makes it sensible to use a straightforward, task-oriented approach in managerial style.[17]

Under conditions of certainty and stability, then, more highly bureaucratic models of organization may make considerable sense.

On the other hand, life in an organizational unit must become more complex in order to deal adequately with an uncertain and rapidly changing sector of the environment. To have more points of contact with the environment, a flatter organization is employed. Formal rules cannot be formulated that will be suitable for any appreciable time period, so it seems better not to rely heavily on them. More of an all-to-all communications pattern is indicated, which can keep environmental clues moving through the unit for interpretation at all points instead of just through superior-subordinate channels. A longer time orientation is usually needed. The growth of this necessarily more complex and sophisticated . . . communication network is fostered by an interpersonal style that emphasizes building strong relations rather than just accomplishing the task, *per se*.[18]

The proposition that organizational forms and processes ought to be reflective of their environment needs to be elaborated in the following ways. First, any "single organization" usually operates in a variety of environments with different degrees of stability and certainty. For example, the development of oil reserves may imply a relatively certain technical environment in the responsible agencies and in the larger technical community, but at the same time there may be "intense" uncertainty or change with regard to the proper rate of development or the extent of foreign involvement. Second, questions of certainty and stability are ultimately subjective rather than objective problems. For example, if a well-defined technology "exists" for the development of oil reserves, but the organizational participants are unaware of the technology, a state of uncertainty exists. Generally speaking, as the level of professionalism increases, subjective uncertainty over means decreases. Third, the level of certainty over both ends and means constantly changes because of learning on the part of organizational actors and because of changes in the "objective" character of the environment. Thus, one could regard changes in administrative arrangements as a series of mistakes or as a relatively rational (although not comprehensively so) sequence of responses to changes in the level of certainty over both the ends and means of development.

In the following section an attempt will be made to show that many of the changes in administrative arrangements in Libya were a relatively rational response to the changing conceptions of development goals and the level of certainty that is associated with the goals. The argument is not that administrative changes in Libya always "made sense," but that they tended to be plausible from the perspective of open systems.

Changing Objectives and Changing Administrative Strategies: An Open-Systems Perspective

A brief outline of the major administrative and economic changes has been provided in Chapters 2, 3, and 6. Briefly summarized, the economic environment in Libya before 1960 was one of abject poverty and economic underdevelopment as defined by any plausible indicator. This picture was radically transformed by the oil discoveries in 1959. Total revenue jumped from $87,730,000 in 1962 to $1,220,000,000 in 1969. These changes are in the context of a country whose two and one-half million people in 1960 had a per-capita income of approximately $100. The dominance of oil in the economy and in government budgets is reflected by the fact that in 1969 oil revenue represented 77 percent of all governmental revenue. Agriculture, which was never able in modern times to support the indigenous population, remained weak by governmental inattention and by migration of the rural population to urban centers. Agricultural imports, based on increased domestic purchasing power, increased from $2,000,000 to nearly $95,000,000 between 1959 and 1968. Also significant was that oil production had little impact on the development of the domestic economy beyond the infusion of large governmental budget surpluses. Natural resources were developed by foreign corporations which depended only marginally on Libyans for manpower or even tertiary support.

The prerevolutionary response to these problems was a development plan which emphasized infrastructure. The priorities of the first plan stressed public works, transportation, communication, and electrification and collectively absorbed about 43 percent of the total allocation. The priorities for the sectors of housing, agriculture, education, industry, and health were 11, 10, 9, 5, and 4 percent of the actual total, respectively."[19] Related figures appear in Chapter 2.

The prerevolutionary pattern of economic development was complemented by a federal governmental structure whose essential function was to allow the maintenance of traditional tribal prerogatives. The federal, geographically decentralized, governmental structure was consistent with the prevolutionary plan for oil development in the sense that the development plan did not require the mobilization of the Libyan public or the application of a certain technology. The relevant administrative structures were those of the oil corporations.

While the prerevolutionary regime was not primarily concerned with domestic growth, there were attempts to provide adequate housing and education with some attention paid to agriculture as well. Ironically, the decentralized, federalized, structure made some sense in dealing with these types of problems because they are relatively uncertain in regard to the precise goals they imply and to the appropriate technology. Further, "human capital" is much more important in housing, agriculture, and education than in oil exploration, therefore adding an additional element of uncertainty.

The prerevolutionary structure also had some potential strength from the perspective of domestic development because of the great interpersonal skills of tribal leaders. The centrality of interpersonal communication in uncertain situations was a lesson the revolutionary regime learned at considerable cost.[20]

The administrative structure of the kingdom suffered from some severe shortcomings as well. If a decentralized structure is to be effective, it must be accompanied by elaborate mechanisms for the integration of the centralized units. Without integration, the effect of decentralization is to assure nonproductive conflict. Attempts at integration initially took the form of rotating the capital among the three federal provinces. Indeed, according to one authority, King Idris "devoted most of his energy to religious and tribal matters and regretted the need to spend much time on affairs of state."[21] Insofar as matters of state received the king's attention, it was not focused on the entire country but on his native Cyrenaica. To these problems of integration were added the clashes of authority between federal and provincial politicians, and a quarrel within the royal family. The lack of effective integration became such a severe and obvious problem that in 1963 the formal governmental structure was changed from federal to unitary. The change in formal arrangements, however, did not reduce the level of governmental instability because the underlying tribal factionalism dominated Libyan politics and administration. Of particular interest here was the fact that those in administrative positions were qualified by their tribal position which typically meant that they were poorly educated and lacked the capacity for long-range planning, an essential integrative device in environments of uncertainty.

The revolutionary regime represented a new set of priorities in several respects, but central was the de-emphasis on the oil sector and the greater emphasis on *balanced domestic* growth. This meant, in general, that "human capital" development would have to be a high general goal with more specific goals dealing with domestic industrial and agricultural development.

The initial administrative thrust of the revolutionary regime was to purge traditional leaders from positions in local and provincial government. Perhaps influenced by Western models of development, the regime replaced local traditional elites with "modernizing bureaucrats." The modernizing bureaucrats generally held marginal positions in the tribal structure but were relatively highly educated, task oriented, and presumably acquainted with rationalized forms of long-range planning. This represented a step forward because it reduced the level of technical uncertainty, but it was also a step backward because it reduced the level of interpersonal competence which is necessary for the effective implementation of programs that require large-scale popular support and operate in uncertain environments. In short, the first set of revolutionary reforms implicitly assumed that local administrative systems should be closed bureaucratic systems which could be sustained through support from the central government.

The failure of the bureaucratic approach presented the regime with a critical dilemma. The modernizing leaders were ineffective because of their inability to mobilize the mass public, but it was also clear that they could not look to the interpersonally skilled and influential traditional leaders because of their lack of sympathy for development goals as conceived by the RCC. The response to these problems, broadly speaking, took the form of the Popular Revolution.

The Popular Revolution was also a step forward in that it recognized the required open character of administrative systems in uncertain environments. The major difficulty of course was that the exclusive reliance on popular committees implied a naive conception of the necessary complexity of administrative systems. The grass-roots approach to local leadership as represented by the popular committees failed to recognize that in addition to public liaison and support, there must be a core technology which is reasonably well developed but which is not allowed to dictate policy outcomes.

The People's Congress movement recognized in its structural arrangements this type of differentiation while at the same time providing for local integrative mechanisms. The congress structure, with membership from popular committees, unions, and the ASU, is an attempt to provide the integration necessary when the subsystems become differentiated. The congress structure provides functional recognition to the open-systems principle that in uncertain environments the primary contingencies faced by administrative systems are those in their environment and that administration as technology must play a subordinate role. The subordination of modernizing officials to the popular committees and relatedly their absence from the Basic People's Congress helps assure that problems of organization and technology will not be the primary preoccupation of local policymakers.

The changes that have occurred in Libyan government and administration since the 1969 revolution have been truly remarkable. Whether the latest set of institutional arrangements will achieve the objectives of mass mobilization and participation in agriculture, housing, and industry remains to be seen.

To this point the major source of institutional change has been Qadafi himself. The missing link in the existing structure is an institutional mechanism for prescribing change. More specifically, when existing arrangements are successful in mobilizing the mass public in support of development goals, it will be necessary to decide, as a matter of institutional routine, if the subordinate role of the bureaucratic elites is appropriate. In short, the level and nature of environmental uncertainty will necessarily change with the success of current arrangements, which in turn will require institutional development and change.

Notes

1. Ferrel Heady, *Public Administration: A Comparative Perspective* (Englewood Cliffs, N.J.: Prentice-Hall, 1966), p. 12.

2. Ibid., p. 23.

3. Wallace S. Sayre, "Bureaucracies: Some Contrasts in Systems," *The Indian Journal of Public Administration* 10 (April-June 1964); 219-229.

4. Monroe Berger, "Bureaucracy East and West," *Administrative Science Quarterly* 1 (March 1957): 518-519.

5. Heady, *Public Administration*, p. 24.

6. Ibid., p. 29

7. Brian Loveman, "The Comparative Administration Group, Development Administration and Antidevelopment," *Public Administration Review* 36 (January/February 1976): 616-621.

8. Ibid., p. 619.

9. Ibid.

10. James D. Thompson, *Organizations in Action* (New York: McGraw-Hill, 1967), pp. 19-23.

11. Robert Packenham, "Political Development Research," in *Approaches to the Study of Political Science*, edited by Michael Hass and Henry Kariel (Scranton, Pa.: Chandler, 1970), p. 172.

12. Ibid., p. 175.

13. J. Eugene Hass and Thomas E. Drabek, *Complex Organizations: A Sociological Perspective* (New York: Macmillan, 1973).

14. Ibid., p. 86.

15. Paul Lawrence and J. W. Lorsch, *Developing Organizations* (Reading, Mass: Addison-Wesley, 1967).

16. Ibid., p. 25.

17. Ibid.

18. Ibid., p. 26.

19. Omar Fathaly, *The Prospects of Political Participation in Libyan Local Government* (Ph.D. diss., The Florida State University, 1975), p. 73.

20. These problems are considered in some detail in Chapters 3 and 6.

21. Elizabeth Hayford, "The Politics of the Kingdom of Libya in Historical Perspective" (Ph.D. diss. Tufts University, 1970), p. 226.

Appendix A

Declaration of the Establishment of the People's Authority

Socialist People's Libyan Arab Jamahiriya, Secretariat of Foreign Affairs, Department of Information and Cultural Affairs. Issued at Gahera in Sebha on Rabi' Awal 12, 1397 H., corresponding to March 2, 1977.

The Libyan Arab people gathering in the general meeting of the popular congresses, the people's committees, the syndicates, the unions, and the professional associations—The General People's Congress.

Starting from the First Statement of the Revolution and the historic Zwara speech and guided by the contents of the Green Book,

Having reviewed the recommendations of the popular congresses, the Constitutional Declaration of Shawal 2, 1389 H., corresponding to December 11, 1969, the resolutions and recommendations of the General People's Congress in its first session held 4-11 Muharram 1396 H., corresponding to 6-18 January 1976, and in its second session held during the period starting from 21 Zul Qeeda to 2 Zul Hijja H., corresponding to 12-24 November 1976,

Believing in what was heralded by the Great First of September Revolution which was triggered by the revolutionary-thinker and teacher, our leader Colonel Muammar Qadafi, head of the Unitary Officers' Movement, crowning the struggle of the fathers and fore-fathers for establishing The Direct Democracy which they see as the final and the decisive solution to the problem of democracy,

Embodying the popular rule on the territory of the Great First of September Revolution establishing the authority of the people who alone should have the authority,

Declare their adherence to freedom and their readiness to defend it on their territory and everywhere in the world and to protect the persecuted freedom-fighters,

Declare their adherence to socialism as a means to achieve ownership for the people and their commitment to achieving comprehensive Arab unity,

Declare their adherence to the spiritual values to safeguard morals and human behavior as well as they affirm the March of the Revolution, under the leadership of the revolutionary-thinker and teacher, our leader Colonel Muammar Qadafi, toward the complete popular authority and the stabilization of society; in this society of freedom, people are the leader and the master in whose hands are the authority, the wealth, and the arms; the March toward finally blocking the road in the face of all sorts of traditional instruments of governing: be they individual, family, tribe, sect, class, Parliament, party, or multiple parties. They also declare their readiness to crush, once and for all, any attempt against the authority of the people.

The Libyan Arab people, having regained, through the Revolution, their control over their present and future destiny, beseeching the help of God and adhering to His Holy Book as the everlasting source of guidance and of the law of society, issue this declaration announcing the establishment of the authority of the people and announce to the people of the world the dawn of the era of the masses:

First: The official name of Libya shall be *The Socialist People's Libyan Arab Jamahiriya.*

Second: The Holy Quran is the law of the Society in the Socialist People's Arab Jamahiriya.

Third: The popular direct authority is the basis of the political system in the Socialist People's Arab Jamahiriya. The authority is for the people who alone should have the authority.

The people exercise their authority through the popular congresses, the people's committees, the syndicates, the unions, the professional associations, and the General People's Congress. The Law defines their function.

Fourth: Defense of the homeland is the responsibility of every Libyan man and woman. Through general military training, the people shall be trained and armed. Law defines the method of preparing the military cadres and the general military training.

The following are the resolutions adopted by the General People's Congress after declaring the establishment of the People's Authority in the Socialist People's Libyan Arab Jamahiriya:

Resolution 1: The General People's Congress announces the establishment of the People's Authority.

Resolution 2: The General People's Congress has chosen the revolutionary intellectual and inspiring leader Colonel Muammar Qadafi as the Secretary-General of the General People's Congress.

Resolution 3: The General People's Congress, in implementation of the decisions and recommendations by the People's Congresses, Trade Unions, and Professional Associations, decides to formulate the General Secretariat of the General People's Congress as follows:

Colonel Muammar Qadafi, Secretary-General; Major Abdulsalam Jalloud, Member; Lieutenant Colonel Abu Bakr Younis Jaber, Member; Lieutenant Colonel Mustafa Al-Kharoubi, Member; Major Khweildi Al-Hemeidi, Member.

Resolution 4: The General Prople's Congress has decided to set up the General People's Committee as follows:

Abdul Ati Al-Obeidi, Chairman of the General People's Committee; Mohammed Al-Jadi, Secretary of Justice; Muftah Al-Usta Omar, Secretary of Health; Ezzedin Al-Mabrouk, Secretary of Oil; Mohammed Al-Tabou, Secretary of Agriculture and Agrarian Reform; Mohammed Al-Mangoush, Secretary of Housing; Taha Ash-Sharif Ben Amer, Liaison Secretary; Abu Bakr Ash-Sharif, Secretary of Trade; Jadallah Azzouz Al-Talhi, Secretary of Industry; Mohammed As-Zarroug Rajab, Secretary of Treasury; Dr. Mohammed Ahmad Ash-Sharif, Secretary of Education; Abdul Majid Al-Gaoud, Secretary of Land Reclamation and Resettlement; Mohammed Al-Faitouri, Secretary of Social Affairs and Social Security; Mohammed Belqasim Al-Zawi, Secretary of Information and Culture; Dr. Omar Al-Magsi, Secretary of Nutrition and Marine Wealth; Mansour Mohammed Badr, Secretary of Marine Transport; Juma Salem Al-Arbash, Secretary of Electricity; Nouri El-Faitouri El-Madani, Secretary of Communications; Abu Zeid Omar Dourda, Secretary of Municipalities; Muftah Kuaiba, Secretary of Youth; Dr. Ali Abdussalam Treiki, Secretary of Foreign Affairs; Milad Shumaila, Secretary of the General People's Committee Affairs; Musa Abu Fraiwa, Secretary of Planning; Dr. Omar Suliman Hammouda, Secretary of Dams and Water Resources; Colonel Younis Belgassem, Secretary of the Interior; Mohammed Attaher Al-Mahjoub, Secretary of Labor and Civil Service.

Index

Index

Achievement motivation, 50
Agriculture, 17
Al Ahram, 1
Almond, Gabriel A., 49, 76
American-Libyan Treaty, 25
Apter, David E., 49
Arab Development Institute, 4
Arab League, 11
Arab Socialist Union (ASU), 41, 70, 86, 87, 88, 92, 95, 99
Area, size, 1
Atomism, 50
Attiga, Ali A., 17

Al-Bakkush, Abdulhamid, 26
Berger, Monroe, 106
Bevin-Sforza Plan, 22
British administration, 12
British Petroleum Company, 20
Budget expenditures, 34, 36 (table)
Bureaucracy, 106, 107, 109, 110, 113

Cyrenaica, 1, 21
Cyrenaica Defense Force (CDF), 25

Detribalization of Administrative Boundaries, 40 (figure)
Development plans: three year, 19, 37; five year, 18, 38 (table)
Drabek, Thomas E., 109

Economic system, 37
Education, 2, 12, 13, 14, 15
Eisenstadt, S.N., 43
Elites, 11, 76, 79, 80, 82, 83, 84, 85, 86, 87, 98
Emile Saint-Lot, 22

Fekini, Muhiaddin, 25
Fezzan, 1, 21
France, 22
French administration, 1

Al-Gaddafi, Wanis, 25
Gaus, John, 106

General Assembly, 22
Grigg, Sir Edward, 22
Gross domestic product (GDP), 16, 20

Hagen, Everett E., 76
Halim, Bin, 25
Hass, Michael, 109
Heady, Ferrel, 105, 106
Health care, 2
Heikal, Mohammad, 1
Higgins, Benjamin, 1, 16, 19
House of Commons, 21
Housing, 2
Huntington, Samuel P., 91, 108, 109

Idris, King, 2, 13, 21, 22, 23, 28
Independence party, 23
Inkeles, Alex, 49
International Bank for Reconstruction and Development (IBRD), 18
Islamic party, 12
Italian occupation, 1, 12, 21

Jalloud, Major A., 21
Jaquaribe, Helio, 76

Al-Kikhya, Omar Mansur, 22
Khal, Joseph A., 49
Koran, 12
Kubar, Abdu-al-Majid, 25

Lawrence, Paul, 110
Lerner, Daniel, 28, 48, 49
Lorsch, J.W., 110
Loveman, Brian, 107

McCelland, David, 50
McKinney, John C., 76
Mabro, Robert, 18, 19, 36
Mahdavy, H., 18, 36
Maziq, Husayn, 25
Military Administration, 21
Modernization, 2, 66, 67 (table), 71, 76, 92, 93
Mufti (juris consult), 11

Nasser, Egyptian President, 24
National Congress Party, 23, 72
National income, 2

Oil, 1, 13, 16, 17, 34
Organization of Petroleum Exporting Countries (OPEC), 20
Othman, Mohammed Bin, 25
Ottoman Period, 1, 10, 11, 12

Parliament, 27
Parsons, Talcott, 49, 76
People's basic congress, 100
People's Committees, 3
People's Congress, 99, 114
People's General Congress, 100
Per-capita income, 16, 1 (1977)

Qadafi, Muammar, 53, 75, 76, 78, 79, 84, 95, 96, 99, 114

Rentier state, 18, 19, 36
Revolution, agricultural, 20; First of September, 19, 36, 91; objectives of, 95, 96; popular, 4, 41, 114; socialist (1969), 1
Revolutionary Command Council (RCC), 75, 79, 83, 87, 88, 95
Riggs, Fred, 49, 106
Royal Diwan, 23
Rural Libyans: atomism, 53, 55 (table); behavior of, 51; evaluation of local administration by, 61, 62 (table); evaluation of mayors by, 60, 61 (table); fatalism, 55 (table); leadership preference among, 59; interpersonal distrust, 56 (table); particularism, 53 54 (table); political development among, 58; religiosity among, 52 (table); tribalism, 57 (table)
Rustow, D., 33

Al-Sakisli, 25
Sayre, Wallace S., 106
Senussi, 21
Sjoberg, Gideon, 49
Sutton, F.X., 49

Thompson, James D., 107
Tonnies, Ferdinand, 76
Traditional society, 9, 10, 48, 49, 50, 76
Tribal status, 2
Tribalization of Administration Boundaries, 40 (table)
Tripolitania, 1, 21

Ulama, 11
United Kingdom, 22
United Nations, 16, 21, 22
United Nations Commission, 2
United States, 22
Urbanization, 15
Urban population, Benghazi and Tripoli, 15
USSR, 22

Verba, Sidney, 76

Weber, Max, 76, 105
Workers' unions, 99
World War II, 21

Zahara, 5
Zavia, 4, 5
Zone committees, 100

About the Authors

Omar I. El Fathaly received the Ph.D. in political science (government) at the Florida State University in 1975, and is currently chairman of the Department of Strategic Studies at the Arab Development Institute, Tripoli, Libya.

Monte Palmer received the Ph.D. in political science from the University of Wisconsin in 1963, and is currently Chairman of the Department of Government at the Florida State University.

Richard Chackerian received the Ph.D. in political science from the University of Washington in 1969, and is currently an associate professor in the Department of Public Administration at the Florida State University.